The Asparagus Wars

Carol Major

Spineless Wonders
PO Box 220 STRAWBERRY HILLS
New South Wales, Australia, 2012

shortaustralianstories.com.au

First published in 2021 by ES-Press
An imprint of Spineless Wonders

Text copyright © Carol Major
Cover illustration and design by Bettina Kaiser and Imogen Rowe

Editorial assistance by Rose Sammut. Proofreading by Susan McCreery

All rights reserved. Without limiting the rights under copyright reserved above, no part of this publication may be produced, stored in or introduced into a retrieval system, or transmitted, in any form or by any means (electronic, mechanical, photocopying, recording or otherwise) without the prior written permission of the publisher of this book.

Typeset in Cochin
Printed and bound by Ingram Spark
Distribution in Australia and New Zealand by New South

The Asparagus Wars / Carol Major
ISBN 978-1-925052-66-4

A catalogue record for this book is available from the National Library of Australia

Author's Note

This is a memoir—a remembering of events from one vantage point. There are other vantage points. Names have been changed because names define in a way that suggest someone or something has been pinned down. Nothing is pinned down, although my sister Alice remains as Alice because there is an essential quality she brings to my life. I can't think to call her anything else. Rudolf Binding, whose letter appears in the prologue, keeps his name too.

I have also combined encounters and events in France, because it was the cross-fertilisation of these conversations and locations that illuminated emotional truth.

The Asparagus Wars

CAROL MAJOR

Letters

Western Front
April 1915   *X*

Marne Region,
north-eastern France
2017

26 September	*1*
27 September	*15*
28 September	*25*
29 September	*39*
30 September	*57*
1 October	*85*
2 October	*103*
3 October	*121*
4 October	*135*
6 October	*145*
7 October	*169*
8 October	*185*
9 October	*203*

Rudolf Binding
soldier on the Western Front
April 1915

It is, indeed, not so simple a matter to write from the war, really from the war; and what you read as Field Post letters in the papers usually have their origin in the lack of understanding that does not allow a man to get hold of the war, to breathe it in although he is living in the midst of it.

The further I penetrate its true inwardness the more I see the hopelessness of making it comprehensive for those who only understand life in the terms of peacetime, and apply these same ideas to war in spite of themselves. They only think that they understand it. It is as if fishes living in water would have a clear conception of what living in the air is like. When one is hauled out on to dry land and dies in the air, then he will know something about it.

Marne Region,
north-eastern France
26 September 2017

My dearest daughter,

    I am writing to you from inside a small cottage in the battlefields of France. Yellow daisies grow along the wall and inside it smells sweetly of drying clay. Sylvie, the owner, has left a book in the sitting room downstairs. There is a fireplace here and narrow French doors that lead into the garden. I can see a patch of rhubarb, a hazelnut tree and fallen pears.

    The book Sylvie left is titled *Traces de la Guerre* and she has offered to take me on a tour of war cemeteries, thinking I'm compiling a history on World War I. But I have declined. I'm only pretending to have that purpose. You would have done the same, brought your paints even if you never picked up a brush.

Why am I here?

Oh, dear heart, why have I been anywhere since your death. With you gone and your brothers having left, I felt like an unlikely soldier who discovers herself miraculously standing when everything else has blown away. Was it me who mistakenly detonated the bomb? Was the shattered landscape all my fault? I became a faceless cleaner who, without emotion, appears to sweep up torn limbs, barbed wire and broken crockery as if they are much the same things. Stops every so often to make sense of a buckle, looks for the belt.

I stumbled into a salon because washing my hair seemed too complicated a task.

'A cut?' the girl asked.

'No, just wash it.'

I left to interview writers at a festival, cue cards on my lap, numb. Helen MacDonald was there. She spoke of her attempt to tame a hawk in the wake of grief. I never line up for book signings but was drawn to her table. 'My daughter,' I began when it was my turn. You had died six weeks ago.

'I give you permission to go mad,' she said, signing her book for both of us. And I did. I went in search of battered places, wild and scarred places as terrible as my heart: the bleak island in the Outer Hebrides in midwinter, the tiny room in Berlin, and to ride pillion on a motor scooter across rice paddies in Kedah. The driver, lean and dark, had stopped to ask if I wanted a lift.

'Where are you headed?'

'Anywhere.'

It was an American, Hermie, who'd enticed me to East Berlin. I'd met him in one of those chat rooms – on painting, I think, because of you. And there he'd been, his photo in black and white. I couldn't bear anything in colour then. Hermie had been a major in the American air force during the Cold War, had studied theology before that, and later left the military to become a minister in a small church, although he'd recently resigned from the position. In Berlin he was writing a play in an artists residency and making small sculptures out of bottle tops and wood – and because of that, because he too was wrestling with war and faith, I flew all the way from Australia to meet him on a railway overpass at nightfall. I couldn't have cared less if he'd buried a knife in my heart. To some extent he did.

Sylvie thinks it sad I will be staying in a two-bedroom cottage alone. 'Why the other room?' she asked. She's very beautiful, sleek and shiny like a strong bird in spring. She is also generous and kind. On my first afternoon, she insisted on taking me to buy groceries in nearby Fismes.

'It is only safe to go in the evenings,' she said. 'The government is putting in a new sewerage system through the villages and the main road is blocked during the day.'

Still, at early evening there were clouds of dust, as if there had been an explosion, as if someone had discovered an undetonated bomb that went off ten minutes ago – all those trucks and men shouting. It could have been the last days of a war, if that's how your imagination runs.

That's how I imagine us, wearing trench coats, waiting out a war. You lie wounded in the next room, while I run through cobblestone streets to buy bunches of asparagus to help you recover. Your little dog, Lulu, puffs behind. I imagine it is the last days of the French Resistance because our drama must be happening in France.

Hermie's play is set in France, and perhaps he will appear despite our falling out. We were supposed to share this small cottage but I have told him he will need to stay somewhere else. I call him Hermie, but we had many names for each other: Red Onion Girl, Milkweed Boy, among others. Hermie stuck because he looks a bit like Hermann Hesse, the thin nose and glasses; he espouses Hesse's philosophy as well. The play he began writing in Berlin has Joyce Kilmer as a key character. Kilmer was an Irish American poet killed in World War I. He's buried in the Oise-Aisne American Cemetery, not far from here.

'Did he think he wouldn't die?' Hermie scoffed. 'He was exempt, you know, didn't have to join up. Did he think he was somehow immune from that probability because he was a devout Roman Catholic convert – or was it American idealism that gripped his throat? We always think we're the good guys, and so like any Hollywood movie we'll win in the end.'

Hermie wanted to see Kilmer's grave and the spot where he was shot. He spoke of this in Berlin and asked if I wanted to come along. I was ambivalent, drawn to Paris instead, but felt if I went to Paris, I would have been stealing that from you as well. I was wearing your long stockings when Hermie asked me. I was lying in his bed.

Do you remember how I tried to get you from Sydney to Paris – how I spoke to travel agents about getting a young woman who couldn't sit up into a jet plane? They said it was possible to take out a row of seats, and I looked into the cost of doing that, the possibility of mortgaging the house, even though I knew the trip would probably kill us both. We went for tests to see if your breathing could handle the air pressure change in a plane. It could, and we were both happy and secretly disturbed. Was it a sign? Did it mean we should go, or did it mean that Lillian's natural therapy regime was working, that you were going to get better and the trip was a mistake? We never admitted what the trip was really about. Rather, you imagined how we would be dressed for the adventure; you bought all those clothes on eBay. It was going to be our grandest creative act.

When you decided to postpone Paris until later, to wait until your stepmother's regime had taken effect, I set about decorating your flat. You chose turquoise and lavender paint and we hung chandeliers in every room. Afterwards, we hosted a cocktail party, the sort of cocktail party people threw in the late forties at the end of another world war. You wore a little black cap with a net, and the following morning I sat in the living room looking out at the plane trees lining the streets beyond: swatches of blue, grey and green. They reminded me of a Pissarro painting. It could have been Paris if I squinted my eyes.

I said as much to the young nurse who bustled in to check your urine charts. She replied that if I was that loose with geography she wouldn't want to be a passenger in my car. The comment reminded me of a question I once asked your youngest brother, Louis. Who would he rather have with him if he was stranded in a desert, his father or me?

Ha! We both know that being with your stepfather is like having an aerial map at your fingertips. He is fit and composed as well. The women who helped with your care always breathed a sigh of relief whenever he appeared in his bicycle gear. It was your stepfather who pedalled off to get replacement pieces for your CPAP breathing machine from a factory the rest of us would have taken hours to find, your stepfather who calmly helped lower you off your balcony in a cherry picker the day the lift caught fire.

But your stepfather is not here, and yesterday I was running low on food. Sylvie said there was a longer back road to Fismes that skirted the construction spots, if I needed to go shopping during the day. But I must have turned left when I should have turned right, because like the road that took me into a field and a pile of stones on the day I arrived, this one turned into a muddy channel between a barbed wire fence and a brambled slope. I was hopelessly stuck, tried gunning the accelerator in reverse and then gunning it forward, but only sunk deeper into the mud.

Your stepfather wouldn't find himself in a situation like that. Never did understand my ability to get lost, to mix up names, even his own – how I kept calling him Jeff when we first met, because Jeff was the name of the other bartender in the tavern where we were working at the time. But haven't I always had this self-styled filing system with names? Apparently, it has something to do with the mind's fluidity with association. For me the name Jeff became associated with order and tasks, and efficiency. Jeff is efficient – seems fitting to call him Jeff now. I still recall how at the end of a shift he would arrange my crumpled tips so the heads on the notes all faced the same way. I thought, now here is someone who practises order. Here is someone with thought-out plans.

Your father is nothing like him. Remember the fridge he bought for you second-hand, the one with glass shelves that cracked and broke? There was a degree of complication in ordering replacements, perhaps something to do with finding the receipt, which in your father's case would have been lost. Whatever the reason, he never got around to completing the task, instead appearing with whacking big bones for Lulu. Heavens, Lulu was getting fat enough as it was. Meanwhile, we had to stack food on top of the crispers and each time anyone opened the door, containers of pureed asparagus and Chinese herbs toppled out.

Do you remember how Jeff didn't come to the rescue that particular time? I think he wanted to make the point that if anything was left to your father, it would never get done. But on the day the broken shelves went beyond a joke and Jeff made a heroic show of ordering replacements himself, your father appeared with a spray of purple bougainvillea, because purple is your favourite colour. He laid it beside your pillow so you would see it when you opened your eyes.

I reflected on that moment as I rocked the car back and forth in the muddy bank, eventually giving up and letting it slide sideways into brambles, where it came to rest against a small tree. The engine died and for some time I sat staring at speckled shadows, my chest heaving in and out. It struck me then that it didn't really matter whether or not I knew exactly where I was on the globe, or if I could get out of this fix. I was simply here, among speckled shadows, and now that the engine had died, it was quiet.

Your room was quiet in the mornings, just the sound of your CPAP machine whirring. I would kneel on the side of your bed and begin rubbing your feet, then the backs of your legs and into the hollow of your lower spine. You would ask me to tell you about the outside world. Had I eaten something nice? Was there gossip I could share?

Today, I will tell you that I eventually did make it out of the brambles. It took some more gunning of the car and a 'Hi-yo, Silver, away!' moment when it lurched up the hill, almost throwing me from the seat. Finally, I was able to get back onto the sealed road, albeit with scratched doors.

I had no idea which way to go afterwards, struck out randomly and turned on to another road that twisted through vineyards and fields of yellow rapeseed until I was on a ridge looking down on the small dormitory village where I'd started out. I was able to see the Romanesque church clearly and the row of cottages, of which Sylvie's is one. Hers is the largest and divided into two separate homestays, or *gîtes*, as they're called here. I'm staying in the smaller side and when I first arrived mistook the entrance for a door to a shed.

Yesterday I parked in the side lane and entered through the rear gate to find a Spanish family about to have supper in the shared yard. Two teenage boys were kicking an inflatable ball back and forth while their mother, a handsome woman with very groomed eyebrows, arranged platters of food on the outdoor table. Her husband – I presumed it was her husband – was leaning against the shed smoking a cigarette. He looked very pleased with himself in his tailored shirt with a scrolled pattern inside the cuffs. Seeing me, he came forward, introduced himself as Blanco, and said Sylvie had told him I was a professor researching the Great War.

I laughed, embarrassed. 'I'm not a professor.'

'Are you English?' he replied, as if this was the alternative. Before I could answer, he went on to say the Spanish were not belligerent in World War I. 'Is that how you call it?' he asked. 'Not belligerent, the country that is not joining in? We were not so nice in World War II. We chose the Germans first and then were not sure.'

His wife moved forward to interrupt. 'Blanco always wants to know everything too fast. But please' – she pointed to the food on the table – 'share with us.'

The platters held squares of toast spread with sardines. The boys swooped in to grab a handful then ran away to kick the ball. This time it bounced through the open gate and into the lane, hitting my car. Blanco shouted at them to be careful, then turned to me. 'Your car,' he said. 'Was there already an accident? The doors are scratched and so much mud. Did you drive far, perhaps all the way to Verdun? If it is a rental, you will need to report a crash.'

I feel terribly raw these days when people take it upon themselves to tell me what I should do. I smiled at his wife, accepted one of the toast squares and shrugged. Hermie had mentioned going to Verdun, although his more pressing quest was to find the location where Kilmer had met his end. It is somewhere on the Ourcq River a few kilometres away. Hermie was very passionate about that battle, would work himself into a frenzy describing how it raged back and forth, and once while relating the details yet again he stopped and said fiercely, 'I'm not a warrior. Neither was Father Duffy, the chaplain in Kilmer's regiment. But he was always right in the thick of it, dragging the wounded to safety, offering the last rites. That's who I wanted to be. I had this deep sense of calling and I've always wanted to know if I'd be up to it when the time came.'

In his small room in the artists residency, Hermie draped me in green gauze, took photographs with a polaroid camera and said my face was so lovely he wanted to hold it in his hands. I remember those timeless days, the red sheet across the window so we couldn't see outside, the top of his desk scattered with beer bottle tops.

'There are so many beer bottle caps in Berlin,' he told me one afternoon when we did venture out into the bright, brittle cold. We were walking on a path that cut through the green space between the outer and inner sections of what was once the Berlin Wall. No-man's land, the site of escape attempts. Children played tag and couples held hands, and the path gleamed with beer bottle tops that had settled in the tar.

On that afternoon, Hermie would call me beloved and take my hand as well, but later he told me that he didn't believe in love. This was after I'd returned to Australia, after he'd sent postcards with tiny sketches of a railway overpass with a heart beneath –after he'd posted a surprise parcel for Christmas that never arrived. He was filled with frustration about not being able to get on with his play. Then came a bitter message about how the Christmas parcel he'd posted had been returned. It was one of his small sculptures.

'Your government refused the box,' came his terse email. 'The customs form said *objet d'art*. Is that code for a refusal?'

It was as if I'd refused his creation myself.

I didn't hear from him for some months and then a long letter appeared in my mailbox, his tiny script written on pages torn from a notebook. *Sorry, sorry, sorry*, although the letter didn't feel sorry. It was seething with anger about women who had not seen his effort, and without saying so explicitly lumping me together with all women, as if we were all one dumb, blind thing. But I think it was the bloody righteousness in his reference to picking up pen and paper rather than the convenience of the digital world – the fact that he'd bothered to fetch an envelope, purchase a stamp – that annoyed me the most. I shot back an email telling him I was too fucking lazy to go to the post office and that women as a whole were not one thing, any more than men. And that his sorry meant shit. However, if he wanted to remain in contact that was fine with me.

He seemed to like that response. We began communicating again, and eventually the excursion to France was resurrected.

I liked the idea of going to a landscape littered with discarded artillery and bones. In Berlin I had walked across the open mouths of the ten thousand metal faces scattered in the Jewish Museum, listening to the clank, clank, clank.

I booked Sylvie's cottage but at the last moment told Hermie he'd need to make his own arrangements. I said this after he was flippant on a Skype call and – oh, I think you would understand. I realised I was reaching a point where I was ready to tell him what happened to us, reveal all those wounds. Do you remember that boy in university – the one who became the centre of so many of your poems? The one who kept messing around with the idea of being with a physically disabled girl? The one who said it was a tragedy that you would never be able to play tennis together, and on that day you shot back that you didn't like tennis, so there was no tragedy in that. As if you'd pine over something you'd never reach for in the first place, able-bodied or not. But I know you pined for some things, even as you sent him packing. I also think you were frightened, the idea of removing that brace, the idea of leaving yourself so exposed. Better to be on your own.

Of course, Hermie was furious. 'Why? Because you want to punish me? World wars are not your particular quest.'

Oh, my dearest, we could tell him something about wars – cold or otherwise. How they start. How they end.

Last night, as evening drained colour from the yard, I had the strangest feeling Blanco knew about Hermie, knew about you. He told me the ground in Verdun was so thick with bones every time a tree fell, skulls and femurs came up tangled in the roots. There was no way of identifying whose bones belonged to whom, and so they were stacked in the basement of the Douaumont Ossuary.

'Impossible to tell the good guys from the bad,' he said, and laughed. Blanco has very shiny teeth.

It was then that he told me about Section E in the Oise-Aisne American Cemetery. 'They bury the bad soldiers there. The ones blindfolded at dawn.' He extended his index finger as if it were a gun barrel and pointed it at his wife. 'Pow, pow.' She flicked him away with a tea towel. Enjoying teasing us both, he said Section E was in a secret place behind the caretaker's office. 'Although that information could be a ruse,' he added. 'Maybe it is in the woods beyond, a mystery like the Catalan fairytale about the Water of Life.'

Have you heard that fairy story, dearest? I hadn't heard it before. It is about an elder brother who sets out on a quest to bring back a jug of this water. He meets a giant who warns him that on his way he will come to a mountain of mocking stones. If the brother is able to ignore the stone's jeers then he will gain what he is after, but if he pays attention, he will turn to stone himself. Of course, as it happens in fairy stories, the stones jeer so loudly he turns to throw a rock at them.

Blanco leaned forward with such a ghoulish expression. 'Maybe you go looking for Section E and turn into stone.'

Was that a challenge to go on a quest myself? Or was it a jeer to see if, like the brother in the fairy story, I would respond? It was unsettling whatever his intention. I did my best to smile in response, said that I was very tired after a long day, and after thanking his wife for the toast, made a hasty departure. Still, I can hear him laughing and the boys kicking that ball.

Marne Region,
north-eastern France
27 September 2017

Dearest it is 3 am. The Spanish family are finally quiet. Half an hour ago I padded downstairs to put on a kettle and be alone with my thoughts, although you, dear heart, are here too. The middle of the night has always been your favourite time, away from the day-time people, you said. Just one lamp and your fairy lights. No need to see every corner of the room. We talked and talked. I can't stop talking to you. I feel compelled to tell you everything that is going on here and everything that went before, some of which you already know, but not how I felt about these things. I never told you how I really felt.

What Blanco told me about Section E is on my mind as well, so that I'm also imagining my scribblings to you might take the form of explanations to a military tribunal –hand on the Bible, swearing to tell the truth. But how to unravel the story of us? It was as if we were all characters in Anne Tyler's novel *The Clock Winder* – the family who kept bringing drama into their lives, winding things up. Too much content. I worry about all the content. Did one thing lead to another? Is that part of the meaning? Or is there no particular thread, just events balancing on each other like a pile of pick-up sticks that ended up with you dead and me no right to grieve?

I was found wanting as a mother long before you came along, four years before I married your father and gave birth to Christopher and then to you. At seventeen I had been one of those teenagers in a home for unwed mothers.

Oh, your father already told you that story when you were very young but in the context that, given I was that sort of woman, it showed how much I cared about you that I'd hung around. Why say such a thing to a child? It was alarming to you and also silenced me, because to explain why I'd given up my first child sounds like a justification and justifications are not the story itself. We were seen – we girls in the home, as juvenile delinquents who should hand over our babies to real mothers, as we could hardly call ourselves that. I see the nurse in the delivery room. She is thin, blond, all tucked in and fastening my hands in straps, my feet high in stirrups.

'Why?' I ask.

'So you won't interfere with the doctor. So you won't touch anything down there. She adjusted the strap around my wrist. 'Haven't you done enough damage already?'

Damage. So much damage. Keep your hands away. I still can't feel my hands at times and was in shock five years later when allowed to walk out of a hospital with Christopher in my arms. He was such a beautiful baby, an easy birth, those harvest days in that small town in Southern Ontario, hayseeds floating in a trance. But you, a daughter, you would not let me escape so easily: twenty-eight hours of labour, as if I had to endure that first, and then your arrival, wild-eyed in the middle of a thunderstorm on a hot autumn night. You tore me. I tore you, your face puffed from the forceps, your dark hair covered in foam. It was an impossible pregnancy. I was still breastfeeding Christopher at the time, hadn't had a menstrual cycle, but during that protracted phase of the moon you planted yourself and clung on. After the birth, you refused to sleep, screamed day and night, only stopped when I picked you up, your eyes fixed on mine, as if you knew, as if you've always known the measure of me.

The local GP arranged to have you admitted to hospital, but paediatricians found nothing wrong, only that you didn't suckle very well. They introduced you to solids – too early, I thought. Later, as you approached your first birthday, it was noticed you didn't smile.

'Such a pout,' said my mother. 'Just like yours when you were a little girl.'

And so it began: first your smile and then your ability to blink. One doctor thought I was making you unhappy, another took note of the constant infections in your eyes and suggested sewing your eyelids half-shut.

Was he mad?

You were fine-boned like me. Fine-boned like your father too, who may have been trying to prove he was equal to big-boned men when he went to Western Australia to work in the mines. It was where he earned enough money to go backpacking through Europe and where eventually he met me, drifting from country to country, sleeping on trains after abandoning university studies. I'd worked hard to get into university, trying to prove I wasn't a delinquent, and because my parents were poor people that had brought their little family from Scotland with such dreams for their children. I felt I'd let them down. But in second year, tired of watching more monied students travel to Switzerland or South America for holidays, I pocketed my student grant and bought a ticket to London, and the train pass. Reckless girl. Opportunistic thief. You would have done the same.

And your father. He was funny. I saw us as two for the road, Huckleberry friends. He came all the way to Canada to see me again. But it's not why I married him. I married him because I wanted to be liberated, and conversely I wanted to be kept safe. Liberated because despite that one mad trip, I couldn't imagine getting out of the east end of Toronto, away from the car yards, the wet slush – and there was your father speaking of the great wide spaces in Australia, properties that stretched over thousands of miles. I dreamed myself Barbara Stanwyck in jodhpurs, bull horns over a great stone fireplace inside the Big Valley mansion, that sort of thing.

Although the blond brick house in the western suburbs of Sydney was nothing like that. I was paraded around like a foreign curiosity, something to irritate your Australian grandfather, I thought, who picked us up from the airport in a Lincoln Continental. He was such a big man back then, came from a grazing family, had bought into an earthmoving business: big trucks, big money. He had a very loud voice. When introduced, he asked if I was from the French part of Canada and appeared relieved when I replied no. After all, coming from that cattle family, he wanted to know what his son was breeding with and told me, as if I had to be educated, that Aboriginal people had weak genes. You could breed them out in two generations. That's why they were taken from their mothers, to give them half a chance. He might have said something else about seeing a calf born with six legs, or perhaps it is my imagination that colours the conversation with this image. That is the other side of genetics. You have to watch for wonky genes.

Why did I think your father could keep me safe? It wasn't your father per se, it was marriage itself. Before any talk of an engagement, I went to a clinic for the birth control pill, a clinic in the same hospital where I'd left my baby behind in a cot. The doctor, liver-coloured, fat hands, said he'd seen my file. 'You've be in trouble before,' he said, as if smelling something awful and tasting it too. He wouldn't have spoken like that had there been a ring on my finger, and I did wonder about myself, this curious, impulsive behaviour that kept getting me into trouble. When my younger brother was an adolescent, he ground the heads off matches, wrapped the dust in foil, lit a string fuse and blew a big bloody hole in the backyard. He's a scientist now. But I was a girl. I remember how strangely safe I'd felt from myself inside the home for unwed mothers: the rules, church at 10 am every day, the doors kept closed. No one outside could see us in there.

Your father was good at drawing lines around behaviour, clear about how people should act. I turned up for our wedding in full costume wearing an eggshell satin dress, cameo pinned at my throat. It was an evening ceremony, March in Canada, the last weekend before Lent. The sky was inky, and the streets wet with sleet. Hooded in a velvet cape I felt like a fairy princess mounting the chapel's stone steps.

We flew to Australia to meet your paternal grandparents the next day. Did I ever tell you that your father's mother was disappointed I hadn't packed the wedding gear? She'd invited the extended family to a barbecue, parrots screaming and fanning their sulphur-yellow crests in the early autumn heat. Had she expected me to appear in heavy satin? I slipped behind the garage, accepted a puff from your grandfather's cigarette when he caught me hiding there.

'Calms the nerves.'

I liked him in some ways.

We took two trips back to Australia. The first one for our honeymoon, and the second when I was pregnant with you. Your father had gained mature entry into a Canadian university, an opportunity not available in Australia back then. He could have chosen almost any discipline with his results – aeronautics, things like that – although had trouble deciding. He liked art, liked design, once showed me a tree he'd drawn. But a degree in art would have been taking rebellion against his father a step too far. Instead, he picked human geography, courses that could lead on to urban planning, the construction industry, something his father could understand.

The student loan and grant offered with his acceptance hardly covered a family of three, never mind you on the way. Your Australian grandparents offered to help. But soon after our return to Canada, their earth-moving business floundered. Months went by before a cheque would arrive. 'Make it stretch,' your Australian grandmother wrote. We were already months behind in rent.

After you were born, I took up waitressing in the evenings. The tips were good, and I didn't need to declare them, which was a bonus because a percentage of my earnings would have been deleted from your father's grant. Oh, I suppose I did need to declare the tips, but who was going to see what I slipped in my pocket? Later, I discovered if I applied to finish my abandoned degree, I could get a student loan and grant too, have access to the cooperative childcare at the university and continue waitressing at night. We still struggled. I see your father and me arguing in the tinned goods aisle of the local supermarket with you and Christopher in the shopping cart. I am shouting that we can't afford a tin of shrimps and he is announcing to those who pass that this is a two dollar and seventy-five cent fight. If they want to see something bigger, they'll need to meet us at the deli bar.

I was good at famine mode, but your father wasn't, and his easy way with money frightened me. My own parents had been shucked from place to place at the mercy of landlords and rising rents. I knew how easy it was to find yourself on the street. Your father first sympathised with my socialist ideas borne from this past but later behaved as if such thinking was hippie dressing. A fashion or a phase, something you played at as kids.

Later, after the marriage ended, and on those occasions where we found ourselves in the same room, he'd be keen to say how lousy Labour was doing, how they were dropping in the polls. The inference being that his kind of people were winning, and my kind of people had lost. I can't say I didn't feel smug when the political tables turned; yet sometimes I wanted to reach across the battlefield to recall a shared memory when we'd been friends: the time when we'd camped in a wood outside of London and woke to hounds barking and men on horseback wearing fox-hunting garb. Did he remember that?

'No, I don't remember anything about my time with you.'

Still, I remember him in those early days with tenderness, his hair chopped like Elton John's, narrow hips, elfin eyes. We are students again and he is rolling out pastry attempting to make a Canadian apple pie. The beans he planted in the student vegetable garden have come up. We've been eating beans for weeks. At the beginning of winter, he tried to make a snowman when there was barely a scraping of snow on the ground and early the following morning he bundled us into a car so that we could see –

what was it we were off to see that day? I forget, but he had to see it.

Marne Region,
north-eastern France
28 September 2017

My darling girl, the sky is dull today, the kitchen a bit cold. Earlier I discovered the small packet of tea bags that I bought on my arrival was empty and that the tea leaves in the tin on top of the fridge were stale. You can steep a tea bag in a cup, but tea leaves are a stretch too far.

    Now the kitchen is a jumble because I pulled out pans and crockery looking for a teapot and can't remember in which cupboards they belong. The upstairs bedrooms are messy too. I've been taking turns sleeping in every bed, unable to decide in which one I feel more settled. The latched window in the master bedroom stares out of the pitched roof at the sky. The bedroom opposite has twin beds printed with blue and red boats, a large square window framing the backyard. Early this morning, I sat in the small sit-tub in the bathroom on the landing between the bedrooms until the water turned stone cold. I was mulling over the story I began yesterday, trying to locate the flash points, trying to come to grips with how wars begin. I'm still mulling over the earlier years, the autumn when you turned one and I decided it made more economic sense to return to university studies. I elected literature, drama and art, hoping to follow with a teaching certificate, a sensible job for a married woman – school holidays at home, that sort of thing.

I was the mother-lady among the younger students – yet, dressed in a box-pleated skirt, I felt twelve years old, the day my periods began, and my mother had shown me how to use a sanitary napkin belt. I couldn't go out on the toboggan hill; I had to wear a skirt. I was wadded, stuffed, kitchen-steamed.

The drama lecturer cast me as Nora in Henrik Ibsen's *A Doll's House*. He had sexy snaky eyes. I was to play the scene next to a boy in a jean jacket who hadn't learned his lines, but I had. It was the scene where Nora's husband, Torval, tells her she's neglected her sacred duty. The lecturer was telling me where to stand, how to hold my arms and then said something about loosening up. I think he also said something about flat-chested chicks and for God's sake take off my cardigan. I don't know what came over me but suddenly I began shouting the lines at the lecturer, Torval's part too. Or maybe I didn't do that. Maybe I shouted something else. What I do remember clearly is him laughing. 'Oh, there you are. Use it. Be that woman.'

By the end of third semester I was wearing shirts tied at the waist, torn jeans and boots. 'What's with dressing like a pirate?' your father asked. I was also staying back to drink Black Russians with the other waitresses after my shift, and popping Valium. The Valium had been prescribed by a doctor at the university medical centre. I was having visual disturbances and moments when I would break out in cold sweats. He wasn't surprised: the study, the hours at the co-op childcare centre, the double-shift waitressing. 'You're having panic attacks. Take a tablet when you feel one coming on.' So I did, and your father liked this because it made me less argumentative, until Valium ended up making me more argumentative. One day during one of our legendary supermarket trips, he told me to take more of them; they were the only thing that seemed to shut me up. I did and ended up in hospital having my stomach pumped, your father shouting at me while I was half-conscious because he was frightened, and the nurse's voice breaking through. 'I don't think she can hear you.'

After being discharged, I lurched around trying to make the house perfect again, bake bread, rush to my waitressing shift to make up for lost wages in that wretched bar wench's costume that never fit properly, my flat chest. One particular night at the end of a shift, as I sat weeping in the change room, one of the waitresses brought me a drink, and then invited me into the bar where I drank three more. I was blind drunk when she drove me and some of the others home, pulling up twice to let me heave my stomach into the snow. Your father was furious when I staggered in the door. Early the following morning, he shook me awake, told me he was taking you and Christopher out for the day and that when he returned, I'd better be the woman he'd married in an eggshell satin dress. Later, when he did return, he said he'd spoken to your Australian grandmother and that she was sending the fare to bring us all home. We'd manage better in Australia. He'd finished his degree, even if I hadn't finished mine.

I didn't put up a fight. He wasn't the bad guy here.

A few days later, he decided it was cruel to stop me completing my last semester. He would take Christopher with him to Australia. I could remain with you and follow at the end of term. I didn't want to go to Australia, to the blond brick house with the grandparents and the bleached light. But I would, because during his absence I would be able to dress anyway I liked and dance on tippy-toes with you and be free. I rationalised that a memory of freedom would be enough to sustain me for my life in Australia. You loved to be on tippy-toe, although one of the waitresses had asked, 'What's wrong with her mouth?'

'Nothing's wrong with her mouth,' I replied. 'I had the exact same expression as a little girl.'

I arrived in Sydney two months later with you in my arms. You wore that farm dress, the one with the little windows that opened on the smock, chickens and cows peeking behind. Your father stood in the arrivals hall, Christopher a little soldier beside him holding a red rose. Next, we were in your Australian grandparents' house. Your father, Christopher, you and me, had been allocated a single room with cowboy curtains, twin beds pushed together and mattresses on the floor. Early the next morning, your grandfather burst in carrying a transistor radio because he was excited with what the talk host was saying, and I discovered I'd menstruated onto the sheets. I came back from the shower to find your grandmother had stripped the bed and there was a bucket of cold water in the kitchen stained pink. She'd unpacked my carry-on bag too: my hairbrush, make-up bag and tablets arranged on the Formica bench beneath delicate voile curtains. The sky beyond was a savage blue.

We stayed in your grandparents' house for three months and then moved to a flat on Sydney's North Shore, one of those functional square blocks with a line of garage spaces underneath. The washing lines were there too, poles poked in concrete and out of the sun. Nothing dried. Still, this was a better address for employment than the Western Suburbs. Your father had a position with a recruiting company then.

Why that? you may ask. I guess it was what was on offer and degrees were scarce in Australia at the time – a degree in anything seemed to guarantee a job. As for me, I scored a position writing promotional material about wildlife and national parks, which was also pretty funny, given I barely knew the difference between a platypus and a kangaroo. I think Christopher still remembers the baby wombat I brought home.

It was July by then, winter in Australia, and the nights damp and cold. Your father and I had little furniture – no bed, just a mattress; turn it over and the underside was covered in mould. A few months later, he was dismissed from his job. He wasn't suited to management procedures and had the clever notion to make mirrors out of old windows and sell them at city markets. Do you remember that vaguely? You were very little. How we spread a purple macramé blanket over a long table at Paddington Markets, brought along pot plants to jazz up the display? You wore green overalls, Christopher blue. The best part was visiting the other stalls, fresh fudge and trinkets, a pencil with a monster's head stuck on the end, your hopeful faces poking up. *Can we, Mummy?* Oh, the heady joy when a mirror was sold.

But your father would be lucky to sell one mirror at each outing and money earned seemed to run so easily through his hands. This frightened me for all the old reasons and we fought like children. We were still children then.

In the midst of our bickering he accused me of having fallen in love with someone else, maybe someone in Canada during those two months I'd been on my own. He would regularly run through lists of names at the university and the tavern where I'd waitressed, although never Jeff's, not Jeff with his freckled face and gee-whiz demeanour. Jeff was as dangerous as breakfast cereal. Then one day his name came up too. I turned scarlet because yes, I did have a fling with Jeff during that last term. Devastated by this discovery and perhaps mortified too, your father shouted he wasn't going to be another statistic in the growing divorce rates. I would remain here as his wife. It was my duty. In the weeks to come he hid passports for you children in a cereal box, cited my name at airports as someone who might try to spirit you both away.

My father once told me there were guys in the merchant marines who got so homesick they almost died. And I have read that during the American Civil War – oh gawd aren't civil wars the worst – some five thousand, two hundred and thirteen cases of chronic homesickness were diagnosed, fifty-eight resulting in death. Three hundred and thirty cases were among Union black soldiers. 'Hypochondria of the heart bringing on lethargy, sleeplessness, stupidity of the mind.' I would sit on a bus travelling up Elizabeth Street in Sydney, close my eyes tight and believe I might open them again to be on tram car in Toronto. Dorothy clicking her ruby slippers. *There's no place like home.*

And of course it wasn't just the culture shock, the palm trees and odd light – your father hated me now. We went to marriage counselling but EVERYTHING was my fault. He checked my every move, took to rummaging through my belongings. It was like being under house arrest, and I was still new in Australia. There was no community barracking for me, except perhaps the marriage counsellor who took me aside and said I might consider going to New Zealand. I didn't need a passport to get myself and the children there – and from there I might be able to fly back to Canada. But if I was caught forging passports for them I might end up in jail.

My sister and I wrote back and forth. You have to imagine a time before Facebook and instant communications – a time when a telephone call chunked up dollars per minute, dropping twenty-cent coins into a pay phone, waiting for the operator to connect. Letters took up to ten days to arrive and another long wait for a reply. I wrote to Jeff as well. In those days it was on aerograms, thin blue paper that folded to become an envelope. I asked for replies to come to the post office box at my workplace, which was near the harbour, ferry horns hooting, the slap of waves.

One day, my sister wrote to say Canadian laws had changed – that despite having lived in Canada for two decades and more, my landed resident status meant I would not be allowed back in the country if absent for longer than six months. And then my mother rang at the foundations's office asking to speak to me. It was Thursday, or perhaps it is just that the word Thursday lies in the same part of my brain as the colour of boiled cauliflower, a greenish grey and dull white. The afternoon sky was that colour. Outside, I heard the lonely scream of gulls. My mother's voice came down the line and I could see her in my mind's eye, her eyes like dark, wet stones. We all share those eyes. I try to conjure up that telephone call now but instead see her standing in the foyer of the home for unwed mothers. She is not allowed to accompany me past the door, and I'm being told not to look back. Or am I seeing her as she was at four years of age, banging on the glass windows of an orphanage in the north of Scotland, screaming for her father who is walking away and has been told not to look back? Her mother is dead. Tuberculosis. He can't look after the four small children and she has been told it will be fine. She will be well looked after and he will do well – although not together. The sky that day is cauliflower-coloured too, just as it is in the scene where she is taking me to the home for unwed mothers. I will be fine. The baby will be fine but not with me. And her eyes are locked on mine, this tough little sparrow of a woman, her wing caught in a fence. What did she say to me over the phone that afternoon in Sydney – the afternoon one day before my six months of absence from Canada would be complete?

'If you can't get the children out then leave them there. No one will hurt them. If you have the means to come back, do it, and we will sort this out.'

It was Jeff who sent the ticket for my return.

What sort of mother leaves her children? But remember I'd had practice, and there has been practice down the family line. Did I decide to go or did my body carry me to the airport? I remember being terrified that your father would arrive to haul me back and so stood on a seat inside a toilet cubicle until the boarding call. I believed my mother. I believed if I could only get back home, sit at my parents' kitchen table, smell Sweet Virginia tobacco smoke wafting from my father's pipe, we could sort out a reasonable solution.

But what is reason in situations like this? In these small hours in Sylvie's kitchen beside a flickering lamp I have been reading about the precursors to war: Germany bearing the deep humiliation of their defeat in 1918 and what that spawned. I have also been thinking of the epic war between the Trojans and Greeks. Was it really about getting Helen back, or the shame that Paris had been able to spirit her away? Menelaus feeling he'd been found wanting – and this less-than thing he'd become could only be destroyed by destroying those who had made him feel this way. At least, that's one spin to put on the behaviour, but I am not in Menelaus's head, and the heart, as it is said, has a private address. As for your father, did he want to destroy me because he felt I'd turned him into a less-than thing? Perhaps he really thought I was dangerous. Perhaps he thought he needed to protect Christopher and you from me.

I entered Canada four hours after the deadline. An immigration officer pulled me to the side, took me into a small office and told me I'd missed the deadline. I wailed how the flight had been held up in Fiji, begged him to listen to my accent, tearfully explained how I still hadn't paid out my Canadian student loan. Where was he going to send me? Scotland? In the end he relented but said I needed to become a Canadian citizen if I ever stepped out of the country for that length of time again.

I see myself sitting at my parents' kitchen table. The telephone rings. I fly up the stairs to my old bedroom, hide in the closet, my heart shaking like a frightened bird in a box. My father is there tapping on the door. 'Darling, for God's sake. What on earth?'

'It's them! It's them!' I scream. 'They are coming to send me back!'

'Who? The phone? It was just the neighbour.'

It took me two hours to come out, creep downstairs. I was a mess for months, took a job in a pancake parlour dressed as Heidi, moved in with Jeff, drank far too much, sent little parcels to Christopher and you.

Just as I was beginning to make a little sense of myself, your father launched a custody suit, painting me as an unfit mother who had relinquished one child and abandoned two more. The papers were served to me in Canada, a court day set in one month's time. My father co-signed a loan for me to attend, and I arrived at Sydney airport to have two men in customs take me into a room and tear my luggage apart. They said there was a security alert about children. I asked if they were able to find any in my bags. Later, I discovered this was a ploy to unsettle me for the day in court. I think it was a lawyer's idea.

What happened next? What happened next? I see myself scurrying up Macquarie Street, a wide avenue with court rooms at the far end and Sydney trying too hard back then to be as slick and cool as London or New York. But the lighting is wrong. The sun is too bright. Everything is too clean. Even the sky. Office workers mill in front of buildings and outdoor cafes as if part of a stage set that can easily be removed. Your father is in front of me in a sharp black suit, as sharp as the barristers coming out of the stone buildings, as sharp as his own lawyer whom I saw earlier, and who looks like a shiny mean dog. My own lawyer has been assigned through a government agency. He has the manner of a public servant, smells of punch clocks, tea rooms, and cardigans, and hasn't been helpful. He only read me the rules of engagement. Your father saw him and laughed.

There is no one to vouch for me in Australia. No one who is on my side, although upon arrival your father has allowed me to visit you and Christopher, even as your Australian grandmother told me I'd lost my right to be a mother the moment I walked out. Christopher clung to me during the visit, begged me to promise I would remain close to him all the days of his life. But these legal proceedings have made me well aware that I cannot fund what is now an international dispute and that you and Christopher will become collateral damage in a war that will rage on and on. So, away from the shiny lawyer, I have offered your father child-support money if he agrees to joint custody, and that I will return to Australia to live.

Your father has countered with care and control to him. This will make me an access parent with visiting rights, but not much more, and it churns like thick mud in my gut because it will be your Australian grandmother who will look after you much of the time.

In the scene that continues to unspool in my mind, your father is taking this agreement back to the court. He walks fast. I'm finding it hard to keep up on a footpath crowded with hawkers selling flowers and office girls in pink lipstick, and businessmen acting as if they are closing international deals when they are not, nor is your father, even as he is acting the part.

Should I have agreed to this deal? Should I have fought harder?

There is a vagrant buried in a doorway, crouched on his haunches, mouth gaping, spit clinging in a stringy web. As I scurry behind your father, this unfortunate man reaches forward and thrusts his hand up my skirt, sudden and fast, then pulls away with glee. Your father turns because he has heard the cry I've made, although he has not seen the vagrant hiding there.

'What?' His mouth in the shape of that word. But I don't tell him what happened because I feel this vagrant in the alcove is the only thing not stage-managed. He has seen through the situation and knows I won't call him out. This is what can be done to women like me. And that is what I am left with in this cold kitchen, still scribbling at Sylvie's table. The bubble in my throat. The feeling I must hold everything there. I cannot speak, only write these things because it is safe now. You are dead.

*Marne Region,
north-eastern France
29 September 2017*

Where are you, darling? In Paris? Here the Spanish family have departed in a noisy rush, leaving me their leftover sardines. I stood on the front step and waved them away, bees humming madly around the yellow daisies and the sky lavender blue. After they'd disappeared, a van pulled up and the driver, a lanky woman carrying an armful of baguettes, rushed down the row of cottages and delivered them to the last door. I opened the kitchen window and called to her. *Vous livrez du pain?* I still haven't been out to buy groceries and have little left but some powdered soup, a half-packet of crackers and a tin of butter beans. But perhaps because of my wretched French accent she didn't turn, and soon was back in the van and driving away. It struck me then that while there was no supermarket in the village, there might be a corner shop that made deliveries.

I grabbed a carry bag and my purse and set off down the lane towards the central road. An open-sided hut sits at the juncture, a circle of broken benches inside that surround a stagnant pond. Further along, stone walls flank the main road. It is lined with footpaths no more than a metre wide at best. I didn't see anyone about, just sleepy cats lolling in the sun and a yellow building with a bell tower on its roof about a hundred metres from a sharp bend. I hoped a shop might be around the corner, but as I drew closer, I saw the bend marked the end of the village. Beyond this point the road widens into a one-lane highway running through open fields. A truck was approaching. Frightened its wheels could mount the footpath when it took the curve, I flattened myself against the stone wall. It entered the turn, wheezing and honking, and taking up the full width of the street. After it had passed, I saw a man flattened against the stone wall opposite, wearing jolly red trousers and cheerfully shaking his fist. He called out something in French, probably something about how ridiculous it was for a large truck to be entering such a narrow street.

Longing for conversation as much as a place to buy bread, I called out *'Est-ce qu'il y a une épicerie dans le village?'*

He called back what I already knew about there being no supermarket in the village and roadwork making it impossible to take a direct route to Fismes during the day.

Alas, there was no local store. There had been one when he was a boy, but with jobs centred in cities now, local businesses had dried up. However, an old woman in the next village sold vegetables she picked fresh from the fields behind her house. There was a small *boulangerie* there too. *Ouverte à toute heure,*' he added and then reverted to English because he could see I was struggling to understand. 'Go anytime. You just need to ring a bell on her gate. She will be pleased you have come.'

I discovered the man's name is Arnaud, and like Sylvie, he wanted to know what I was doing in a dormitory village at the beginning of autumn. Few tourists came at this time of year. I gave my usual spiel about being interested in the Great War.

'Aha,' he replied with satisfaction. 'The local mayor isn't interested in history, but it is what draws people. I organised a display in a local park about Howard Houston, the American soldier who was shot nearby. Have you seen the washhouse?'

'The washhouse?'

'The Houston family wanted to do something for the village. They dug wells and built a washhouse back then. *La hutte. Là-bas.*' He pointed in the direction from where I'd come. 'A place to wash themselves and their clothes. They had no running water or plumbing after the war.'

I realised he was talking about the open-sided hut.

Arnaud was kind enough to sketch a map to the *boulangerie* and the house of the old woman who sold vegetables. He also said I must meet his wife, Carole. Carole is a keen history buff and has organised a group that meets on weekends to clean tombstones. Arnaud said she would welcome me coming along.

I did find the old woman's house after only two mistakes. She appeared when I rang the bell. She is very stooped. I suppose it's from years of gardening. The vegetables are stored in a caravan parked in her drive. Most likely she picks them during the cool morning hours: small baskets of onions, tomatoes, leeks, and a few new green beans, just a handful. I bought the beans and imagined bringing them to you. I'd put them through the juicer with the asparagus or roast them lightly in the oven with olive oil and garlic and blend them after that.

Lillian believed asparagus could cure you. Later, she added a mixture of cottage cheese and flaxseed oil to this diet, and later still fish cartilage powder that she ordered from America, and Chinese herbs. I always followed her instructions to the letter. Even as I write this, I imagine putting on my coat, clipping on Lulu's lead. We will run under plane trees, under terrace balconies, past the statue in Union Square. We will run to the market in Pyrmont to buy bunches of asparagus. We will run and run and run.

Dearest, it is later in the day. I have sat down to write to you again fearful you might be worried about me. I'm fine, really. I made a stir-fry out of the vegetables and ate them with a bit of cheese and a slice of baguette. I did buy a baguette today as well. The table is a little tidier. I've stacked the pages I have been writing to you in a neat pile. Do you know that the British Postal Service delivered some two billion letters during World War I and that in 1917 alone over nineteen thousand mailbags crossed the English Channel each day carrying letters to troops on the Western Front? I've been reading some of those letters – this one from Teddy Ashton, although he wasn't on the Western Front. He wrote it in May 1916 from HMS *Albemarle* to his beloved Gertie.

Dear Gertie, I have written two or three times recently so you may get them together. We have been very busy for the last few weeks and have got through a great amount of work. We are much better off again as regards potatoes and other food stuffs for we have had a great quantity of stores. I fancy we shall be here for some time yet, anyway it looks like it with such a quantity of stores aboard. You will see I am telling you the same things over and over again. At least I know I have told you them once or twice but everything about is all of a sameness kind of thing.

My darling girl, I also feel I am telling you things I've told you before but with a desperation to remember them more clearly myself. Teddy Ashton was in Russian territorial waters when he wrote his letters. There was a terrible blizzard. I imagine that thick white sky and how I haven't seen a blizzard in a very long time. Sometimes there is light flurry of snow around my cottage in the Blue Mountains, but it melts quickly, doesn't pile up and up like it did in Canada. In the winter after you turned one, some forty inches (over one-hundred centimetres in today's measurements) blew into drifts and completely covered the front door. We had to poke our way out. The following winter, when your father went back to Australia with Christopher, I pulled you to the childcare centre in a toboggan. The car had gone belly up. I love the smell of snow coming, the muffled world, the puff, puff, puff of my breath as I pull the toboggan cords, turn to see your rosy cheeks.

After the custody case, I knew I would be saying goodbye to all of that, to myself in some ways too. No one would know me in Australia, and by that time you and Christopher had become deeply entrenched in your grandparents' world. I so wanted to have you back in Canada just for a little time to lodge into your memory images of mittens drying on radiators, Christmas lights in late indigo afternoons, my mother lilting carols in the kitchen. My father packing tobacco in his pipe.

Your father had softened by then, some of his rage spent. 'Don't make me look like a fool. If I agree, you must bring them back.'

Do you remember that trip? A chaperone came with you and during those weeks I took Christopher and you to see *The Nutcracker Suite* at Massey Hall and the Santa elf displays in the Eaton's department store windows, and to buy a real Christmas tree on a cold afternoon for all the wintry Christmases you and your brother might never see again. I also made an appointment at the SickKids Hospital in Toronto.

During the months in Australia when the marriage between your father and me was crumbling and finally cracked, we were becoming increasingly aware that your lower lip had developed into more than a pout. This also caught the attention of the woman who cared for you and Christopher while we were at work. Now I'm trying to remember, had she read a story about a microsurgeon who repaired damaged facial nerves or did she know him? Did I consider your facial nerves might be damaged? There had been that difficult forceps birth.

Your father and I made an appointment and I fled Australia before the appointment fell due.

The children will be fine.

The children will be fine.

No, they are not.

I am with you in a clinic at the SickKids. My mother works as a filing clerk in the record-keeping department in the basement. What am I playing at? Am I thinking the paediatrician is going to prescribe an ongoing treatment that can only be undertaken here?

He turns your chin gently from side to side, raises your arms. 'Her shoulders are slightly weak.' He smiles kindly at you.

Moths flutter in my brain, their wings holding me in a hushed tunnel. The slightly weak shoulders hardly register. Of course they are weak. I'm not a champion at tennis, was always last in my high school class to be picked for the volleyball team, their big muscly arms. His voice breaks through. 'There is a possibility your little girl might have Moebius syndrome, a condition affecting both shoulders and face. Are you returning to Australia?' His face is puzzled; why had I asked for an appointment if I was going to relocate? 'You should seek a complete diagnosis there.'

Outside the hospital snow falls again.

I have already told Jeff we would need to part. If the choice is between him and my children, I have to be with them. Now he tells me he wants to come with me, that he loves me, tells the immigration authorities the same thing. Tells them about my situation and how I will need his support. He has become my hero, my knight in shining armour. Like the story I spun around being Barbara Stanwyck riding across the Big Valley Ranch, I spin a story around him too.

We land in Australia on Valentine's Day. High summer. Your father is coming to meet us at a Maroubra motel. But I have no memory of that. Just tiles in the motel's shower recess, a high window and then a complete slide missing from a projector's carousel wheel.

Ironically, Jeff and I rented a flat close to the block where I'd lived with your father. Jeff found a job as a consultant to the restaurant industry, the financial side of things. I worked as a journalist in the healthcare field. Every second weekend I caught public transport to collect you and Christopher from your grandparents' house. I also returned to take you to dance lessons on Monday afternoons. My employer gave me a half-day off.

Do you recall any of this? I still feel wretched that I didn't think to ask Christopher if he would like to take dance lessons too. I remember him unexpectedly saying he wanted to be one of those men twirling a cane and tap-dancing in a top hat and bow tie.

Several months into this arrangement, your father told me to forget about support payments. He would rather I took you every weekend. He needed time to concentrate on building a business of his own.

I loved having you but it was a lonely gig. Weekends are busy times for restaurants and Jeff was frequently away. I also found it difficult to make friends with other mothers. My situation was awkward to explain. What mother becomes the access parent? What on earth had I done wrong? Then during the week I wasn't a mother. I was a woman working in an office, free to go out at night, although not with Jeff. It wasn't unusual for him to return at 2 or 3 am. Without him I didn't feel inclined go out with single colleagues at work. Was I single? I felt caught between two worlds. Often it was me alone in a playground on the weekends, pushing you and Christopher on a swing.

One Friday evening, your father rang to say that rather than me taking public transport, he could drop you both off. He appeared the next morning, a slight smirk on his face as he took in the location. The irony was not lost on him either.

'Where is he?' he asked, stepping out of his car.

'Working.'

He unbuckled your seatbelts, then hesitated and turned. 'Want to come with us instead?'

I think he said something about going to a quarry. Something to do with his new business, something to do with him pricing the cost of stone. You looked up at me with your sweet round face. Christopher's eyes were wide. I was flooded with the joy of being the circle of us again. It didn't matter that the business of marriage had failed.

The trip took us west. We reached the Blue Mountains, the place where I live now. Your father and I sat in front of a roaring fire in the Hydro Majestic Hotel while you and Christopher played at our feet.

It was in the ruddy comfort of that room, cheerful hikers at the bar and through the window the Megalong Valley gleaming in the sinking sun, that your father told me about Lillian, this woman he'd met who was elegance itself. Oh, the warmth of that late afternoon, the fire, your father's sweet desire to get it right with this young woman. He'd invited her for dinner. What should he cook? I think I offered a recipe for fish.

Some weeks later, Lillian appeared at my door with your shoes. Your father had forgotten to pack them, and she had come all that way. She had such beautiful feet. That's what I remember, those slim feet in slip-on shoes, her gleaming dark hair and elegant Modigliani face.

I also remember around this time, or perhaps a little earlier, your father suggested Christopher and you might come to live with me full-time.

There is danger in triumphalism. And I did feel triumphant, because every time I picked you up from your Australian grandparents' or rung to confirm arrangements, your grandmother would say something veiled and snarky, something that implied she had the power and could twist me any way she liked. Now I had this in my pocket and so it happened that one day – I think it was during a phone call with her to make arrangements, and during which she made comments about her health and how looking after you both was wearing her thin – I shot back that she wouldn't need to be so tired in the future, because you and Christopher were coming to live with me full-time.

Your father rang soon after, screaming I'd destroyed that plan. I suppose your grandmother had screamed at him. Later, I was told I couldn't take you to dance lessons. Lillian wouldn't suffer me making cameo performances as a mother. What brought her into the fight?

It is difficult to plot in sequential order what happened next. Does it matter terribly? Only that they did happen. It was either a little earlier or later that your father and I attended a second appointment with the microsurgeon together. I don't recall going together being overly fraught, and the microsurgeon seemed pleased to meet me, having met your father before. He said something about my facial structure having similarities to yours. Did I say something to him about the paediatricians in Toronto mentioning Moebius syndrome? I'm not sure, think he dismissed the idea, but do remember him booking you into the Children's Hospital in Randwick. He needed muscle biopsies to make sure nothing else was going on. The eventual plan was to graft nerves from your feet into your face.

Jeff and I had recently moved to Randwick. Do you remember that semi-detached house? We papered the second bedroom bright orange. Christopher and you helped apply the paste. Later, I lost the rental bond for doing this without the owner's permission, and later still for painting a moon and stars in the alcove where we placed Max's cot. But that was much later. In this moment in the microsurgeon's office I was simply pleased that the move to Randwick meant I could be close to you for the biopsies and other tests.

But a few days prior to your admission your father rang. No preamble, simply, 'I've drawn up a roster for her hospital stay. My parents don't want to run into you. They don't want to see your face.'

'But I live so close,' I replied. 'What if someone can't get there? I can slip out when you or your parents come in.' I couldn't bear the thought of you being alone. But I didn't argue. My face. My awful face that can't be seen.

You were left alone. I came in to find you distressed in a cot. You'd been distressed for some time. When the nurse said you were being discharged a day early, I packed your bags, lifted you out, and signed the discharge forms. The nurse called out as we were leaving, 'You're going home with Mummy now.'

But I don't want to make out that I was saving you. I only wanted to hear those words and pretend.

You can only imagine how it went when your father and grandparents arrived the next day to find an empty cot. Me all wide-eyed when your father turned up at my door. I feigned innocence, said I thought he'd been told and was just trying to help.

It's a wonder we went to hear the results together. I can't recall if the appointment was in the microsurgeon's office or if we were directed to see the muscle specialist. What does stick is a memory of the office being white and that it had the same cold lighting as the inside of a fridge, same humming noise too. Yes, that's what I remember, something hummed. I sat on a chair on the left. Your father sat on a chair on the right. We were informed that you had a special form of muscular dystrophy. It had begun in your face and progressed to your shoulders. What it would mean for you was unknown. It was suspected the disease was the result of a spontaneous mutation, as neither of us showed any signs, and there was no family history.

Dearest, I have sat in a room with the same cold light and chill odour of a refrigerator before. It was a social worker's office, the adoption consent form on her desk. She handed me a pen. The agreement stated that I would never attempt contact with my first-born child or seek after his welfare. While every part of my being wanted to scream, I knew I was supposed to accommodate this calmly. This was for the good of both of us. There was no mention of the loss to be endured, only a minor adjustment in my thinking to be made. So, in that office where I was told about you, I also sat prim and accepting, adjusting to the idea that you might not be a ballerina, even as I couldn't feel my hands, or my breasts, or my feet on the floor. Although I did hear your father screaming. 'A wheelchair! A wheelchair! Are you telling us she's going to end up in a wheelchair?'

I turned to see him staring down that bleak tunnel, feeling he was willing that to happen. He was already there. Why live there when we were here? Why live there when you were still dancing tippy-toe in your farm dress with happy chickens and cows?

Jeff and I married in the new year. No engagement ring, no knee-bending thing. I think we had an argument, made up, then heard his family wanted to visit Australia. My parents had been saving up for a visit too. We had the right people for a reception line. Do you remember being the flower girl? The wedding arrangements were so casual. A dress on sale for me; the Greek neighbour playing his accordion at the reception; friends making a three-layered sponge cake, covering it in marzipan and decorating it with a bow. Christopher was the ringbearer, holding the cushion out on an extended hand from the moment he stepped out of the car. And you, you in an expensive designer dress, pink and intricately smocked with a trimmed underskirt. Your outfit was the only part of that wedding I wasn't the least bit casual about. And we danced. I remember dancing with you, how you curtseyed in that pretty pink dress. Five years old.

Shortly before the wedding I'd spent two days in hospital after experiencing gripping stomach cramps. A doctor took Jeff to one side when he heard about the hasty wedding plans. 'That woman is totally infertile,' he said. 'You should know that now.'

Hardly a month out from stopping contraception, I was expecting Max.

How much later did the affidavit letter arrive through a lawyer claiming I wasn't paying what had been agreed in terms of custody support? All payments accrued must be received in full. The verbal agreement. What had happened to that? When I asked your father, he shrugged, his eyes flat, and said something to the effect that the conversation may have occurred but there it was, nothing in writing. Oh, this had been brewing. Someone had discovered a receipt for a pair of shoes in the bag I sent back with your belongings. I had my hair cut, had it cut again because the pregnancy was turning it to straw. But these things were perceived as me living the high life while others were struggling.

I panicked. I think I got all hoity-toity and said I was holding those payments in a savings account for Christopher and your education. The implication being that I was the more responsible parent who thought of such things. But I had done nothing of the kind. I'd spent it on furniture for your room, outings – yes, the haircuts and shoes and the wedding clothes. Of course, the lawyer wanted to see this savings account and I can't remember exactly what happened next, only an image of myself holding a telephone receiver next to my ear, the kind of telephones used back then with a cradle for the receiver and a coiled cord that didn't stretch as far as you needed it to go – stretching, stretching to where I was crouched on the floor. It was Easter. Your access visit was cancelled. All those chocolate eggs melting in hiding spots. Weekly visits were cut back too, and another court appearance set.

I went to see a lawyer, a man who'd studied history before entering the profession. I told him I didn't want a legal battle; I wanted counselling. Couldn't both sides talk this through? It seemed to me that legal battles were more about manoeuvring painted military figurines on green felt cloth or playing chess. Winning at strategy and little else. Did I suggest Jeff attend the counselling too? The lawyer had met Jeff. I have a memory of the lawyer replying, 'best not' – a flash in my peripheral vision now as I scribble these words. People seeing something I'd missed, something I didn't want to see, like your scapulae unhinging when I lifted your dress over your head to pop you into a bath.

I think it was just me and the lawyer in the courthouse that day. I was very pregnant with Max. My lawyer didn't come into the counselling room, just took me to the door. Lillian and your father were with their lawyer too. I think they were poring over my bank statements. Lillian didn't look herself. As for the scene inside the room, my memory assembles everyone else standing and me in a chair. Your father and Lillian loom, their flushed faces spitting out something to do with me not having breakfast cereal in my cupboards, something about my cupboards being bare. Oh gosh, I can't assemble what they said exactly, only the sense of it being that I didn't run a normal household. And then came the words. 'That woman is not fit to be with children. When that baby is born it should be taken away.'

The counsellor took a sharp breath, turned to me. 'I'm sure you have your side of the story.' His voice was kind.

But there it was.

I am back at the home for unwed mothers, a staff member ordering me in from the front step where I've been chatting with another resident in the afternoon sun. The neighbours complained because they saw us. I am back at the prenatal clinic with an intern poking fun at me as he looks between my legs. I am with passengers on a tram on the return trip muttering and turning away, and always in a delivery room with a nurse strapping my wrists. 'Haven't you caused enough damage already?'

I turned to the kind court counsellor. 'Nothing,' I replied. 'I have nothing to say.'

Marne Region,
north-eastern France
30 September 2017

Dearest,

I have just returned from Arnaud and Carole's cottage. I thought I would take up the invitation to clean tombstones but by the time I got to their home it was threatening rain. Carole brought out historical maps and books instead, and invited me to dinner: braised veal with raisins, a fennel and pear salad, and apple tart for dessert. Arnaud insisted on walking me home afterwards and went to great lengths to make sure I locked my door.

'You are too careless,' he said, showing me how to secure the latch. I think he knows I am not here simply to research

World War I history, but after something darker and more complex. It is pitch black outside now, clouds covering the moon and stars. Earlier in the day, I mustered the courage to drive to the Oise-Aisne American Cemetery but turned the car back around when it came into view. The grounds are so ordered, too spick and span and standing to attention. An American flag fluttered on a white pole. I was holding something quite different in my imagination, Kilmer's grave on a lonely hill and Section E – for that I'd imagined burnt trees, still smoking like spent matchsticks, the flat markers beneath, and maybe me turning into stone. Something had to be revealed by going into that space. But the setting – it looked like a postcard, too brightly lit.

I did come across a more likely burial ground on my return. There are so many, this one in a grey wood surrounded by a low rubble wall. Stone crosses bore weathered inscriptions: *Ian 18 years. Alasdair 19 years*, and often underneath, *love Mum and Dad*. Those losses happened almost a century ago and yet they could have been families today – footsteps tumbling down the stairs, *Mum, Dad, going out now*, and the voices in return, *don't forget your scarf*.

I read up on the Oise-Aisne American Cemetery on my return – typical me, looking at websites after the event, rather than preparing for the trip. Like other military cemeteries, it was built to consolidate remains of soldiers who'd been buried close to where they were killed. The remains in Section E have been dug up from other locations too: bodies of murderers and rapists, and Private Eddie Slovik, who was shot for desertion. Apparently, he took the sentence calmly, saying the army needed an example and he was it, although his death didn't act as much of a deterrent. As another deserter reasoned, 'Well, buddy, what difference does it make whether the Germans kill me, or our own army shoots me? I'm still one dead son of a bitch.'

There are no crosses in Section E, just flat markers sequentially numbered, so it's impossible to know who is who without having the key. Although I did learn none have Eddie below. He was dug up yet again and reburied in Detroit. I can hear you laughing already, something darkly comic in all this moving of decaying bodies around. Remember that mug you had with a cartoon of the boneless chicken farm, chickens wobbling along on crutches and others flopped in wheelchairs? You laughed and laughed and laughed.

But let me tell you about Arnaud and Carole's cottage. It has a sign on the entrance pillar: *Push the buzzer below and if it doesn't work try ringing the bell closer to the door.* There are signs leading to the garden as well: *Watch for Elves, Watch for Bears*. The decorations reminded me of Wobbies World, a funny little amusement park outside Melbourne where I stopped with you and Christopher late one afternoon. Do you remember it? We'd hoped to go for a ride on Puffing Billy, an old-time steam train. But I got lost, couldn't find the station, and drove around and around until we found ourselves in a scrappy paddock. The owners had built a story world out of old transport vehicles. I seem to remember some sort of farming implement painted to look like monster teeth, a broken train carriage that sold meat pies. There was a helicopter too. Christopher wouldn't get out of the driver's seat. We were amused for hours.

That was when Jeff was transferred to Melbourne for several years and I agreed to go with him because the fighting between Lillian, your father and me had grown too fierce. Rather than weekend visits, you and Christopher flew down from Sydney for the school holidays. The warring adults didn't need to see each other, just drop you off at the airport and pick you up.

This was less fraught than those awkward pick-ups every second weekend with people shouting if I was late with your return or had lost your hairclip, forgotten a sock. Me shrieking at Christopher because he'd begged to leave a smidgeon later to hit a cricket ball one last time. 'See! See! I told you this would happen.'

His little frozen face.

I see you one particular afternoon, all of six years old, beside Christopher in the back seat of my car. Children enjoy stirring the pot and you were smart enough to pick up the situation between the adults, clever enough to know which buttons to push.

'We painted pictures of our mothers,' you piped up, as I approached your father's house. He'd built a home of his own by then, had married Lillian. 'They've put them up in the school hall. It's closed up on the weekend, but you can see my painting through the window.'

I hadn't dared ask to meet your teachers or come to a parents night.

Christopher began kicking his feet, screaming we might be late. I thought he was jealous. But when I pressed my nose against the classroom window, the painting wasn't of me; it was a painting of her, Lillian, sweet and groomed with a bow in her hair, and Christopher shouting, 'I drew a picture of you, Mummy. I drew a picture of you!'

You weren't always kind. You weren't a saint, but I would have done the same, played both sides against the middle, made me work harder to prove I loved you the best, kept the other side on their toes as well. By then I was flipping cartwheels to show I loved you the best, as if one kind of love is better than another.

Arnaud and Carole's home smells of clay and straw, and like Sylvie's cottage, the sitting room is below ground. The light is pigeon blue. Carole was sad I would not see the tombstones but was eager to unfold a map showing where they were. She is angular and dark, and wore square-framed glasses that made her eyes look as though each one was inside a small television screen. She thought I'd been touring all over the place and asked if I'd been to the cathedral in Courville.

Sylvie drove through Courville when she took me to Fismes, but I hadn't paid much attention to the signs on the road.

'You must see it,' Carole said. Her English is very practised and precise. 'There was once a castle next door and a connecting bridge that is gone now. Bombed. So many things have been bombed. Archbishops walked back and forth in the earlier centuries without having to rub shoulders with the peasants below.' She bubbled a laugh that was close to a snort.

I thought of the time my sister Alice and I took you to Scotland and couldn't get you inside St Columba's Chapel. The ruins sat on a bald rise, the entrance blocked with rubble, the roof gone. I hoisted you out of the wheelchair onto a window ledge and stuffed you through the opening. Alice stood on the opposite side and lowered you onto a tartan rug. I remember the sky was all cloud-scratched that day and your hair flew wild and free like Flora Macdonald, your face just as bold and fey.

'These are not things you are interested in?' Carole asked, and I realised I'd fallen silent again for too long. 'I was only thinking about war,' I replied. 'The bombed church. So much has been destroyed.'

'*Bien sur*. The battleground of Belleau Wood is very near to our village. The American Cemetery overlooks the point where the German advance was stopped. Here, here,' she said, pointing to her map.

I thought of Hermie and Joyce Kilmer. Yes, the Battle of Belleau Wood, where the tide of war was turned.

'Joyce Kilmer was killed in that war,' I said.

'Who?'

'The American poet. He wrote the verse about never seeing a poem as lovely as a tree.'

It was then that Arnaud took me into the garden. He wanted me to see it before the rain set in. It was there that I asked him about Section E. Had he heard of it? I asked the question casually, as if I was barely interested, only that the Spanish man who had stayed in the *gîte* next door had brought it up. Was it in the Oise-Aisne American Cemetery or somewhere else?

We were standing near his ancient cherry tree. Many of its leaves have curled and dropped, although autumn is barely upon us. He turned, suddenly thoughtful and serious.

'A graveyard for the bad soldiers? Why would he say to look for this place?'

I shrugged, then bent to study the fallen leaves so he couldn't read my thoughts. Arnaud seems to know everything about the area, but clearly not this place.

Do you think Hermie has heard of Section E? It is in the same cemetery as Kilmer's grave. Do you think he might be in France? I could write an email but can only imagine his response. *What? Do you want a selfie beside the graves?* But maybe he wouldn't say that. I don't know everything Hermie thinks, any more than he knows everything about me. I've never told him about you.

Arnaud thought my attention was on the leaves. 'There was little rain at the right time,' he explained. 'The summer was too hot. The tree has been there for over a hundred years, but I don't think it will make it to another spring.' Arnaud's nose is squashed in the middle, like a boxer. I haven't asked but wonder if it was a fight or a motorbike accident. He did tell me earlier that he used to ride a motorbike, was a bit of a punk. '*J'étais cool à l'époque,*' he said, tossing his head and thrusting his hips.

He also said he'd been a keen photographer in those earlier years. 'Not so much now. But almost *un professionnel.*'

That self-mocking toss of his head again. Now he is a retired engineer. I forget the particular area but think he mentioned something about public works, which would explain why he'd been so impressed with the washhouse – the wells the Houston family dug and then plumbed into the village. Another grateful family built something similar in Courville. Arnaud said I must see it too. *'C'est plus grand,'* he said. 'Made out of stone.'

We had supper in the low-beamed dining room, chalky walls peeling under distemper paint and glimpses of pots hanging from rafters in the kitchen beyond. Carole wanted to hear how I had been spending my days, still under the impression I'd been driving far and wide. I equivocated, told her about the little cemetery I'd found in the wood.

'Ah the Buzancy Cemetery,' she replied, when I described the setting, and began recounting the battles in which the soldiers had fallen. 'The village of Buzancy was reached on the twenty first of July 1918 and then the Scots came two days later.'

Arnaud was watching me closely, perhaps something in my eyes, and turned the conversation to the new French president. He put down his fork, stood up and puffed out his chest in a parody. 'They have named him Jupiter,' he said, strutting around the room. 'Here I am on my victory walk through the Louvre's esplanade. Strike up Beethoven's *Ode to Joy*!'

Carole told him he was being silly, then said again that I must see the cathedral in Courville. 'I'm not religious,' she said, 'but it is very historical. *En tous cas*, the French clergy were not exempt from military service by the time of World War I. Separation of Church and State was established in 1905.' Her face was triumphant, all of these facts recalled.

Arnaud pushed a slice of pear around and around on his plate, glanced up at his wife. 'The rules of religion do not always search for the true faith. *Les choses*, the things, *plus grandes que nous*' – he turned to me – 'bigger than us.' He turned back to Carole. 'Do you remember that friend who was told as a little boy that his mother would recover from an illness if he prayed? She never recovered although he prayed and prayed. He always felt he did not pray hard enough. But what should he have prayed for?'

'What a silly, sad story to tell,' said Carole, reaching to lift his plate. 'And I am taking your food away if you are only going to play with it.' She turned to me. 'Many priests who did not need to go to war in other countries still picked up guns. They stood in their pulpits and encouraged killing, telling the congregation that people, both good and bad, must be killed to save the world.' She blushed then. 'Oh, I am sorry. Are *you* religious?'

I shook my head, thinking of my great-grandmothers, one Catholic, the other Protestant, which was why after arriving in Canada my parents joined the Anglican Church where we could be as Catholic as possible while remaining on the Protestant side. One joined a church in those days; it was expected, although my mother rarely attended services. She stayed home with your uncle, a baby then. It was peaceful with the rest of us gone. She called them her God-given hours.

Later, my father's enthusiasm fell away too. He would begin the journey with my sister and me dressed in Sunday hats and prim white gloves, but we'd end up in the local ravine playing with sticks and leaves. We didn't admit this to my mother. She knew, but the pretence continued, a tacit agreement similar to saying you believed in Santa Claus or the Easter Bunny long after you were old enough to know, because these things held such charm. Nevertheless, I was at an impressionable age when we did go to church – the hymns, the call and response chant of Holy Communion, the smell of wooden pews – so that I still bow my head when facing an altar. And on the day you began using a wheelchair, I ran into an Anglican church and threw myself down on a pew. I so desperately wanted to explain myself – why I had left the family home when you were a little girl, how I didn't know you had a mild form of disease that would gradually eat your muscles away. I would have happily been dragged up to the altar in sackcloth and whipped. All the shame. I've read guilt is the fear the bad things you've done will be exposed, but shame is the feeling there is something wrong with you. While I was kneeling, the minister came to the part in the prayer book about 'thou being an all-seeing God', and then, 'not weighing our merits but pardoning our offences'. I took some relief in those words. The idea of there being a something that had seen everything and perhaps there was no need to explain anymore.

I went back to that church for some months, looking for understanding, but there were too many stories about women and children I couldn't swallow, one from the Old Testament about men under a God-fearing ruler whose constituents began marrying pagan women living nearby. I imagined cheerful creatures who danced a lot, wore ankle bracelets, hoop earrings, worshipped the sun and moon. Apparently, God whispered in the ruler's ear that these men must denounce their wives and send them and any offspring away. The alternative was to face His anger (capital H), which would not be pretty at all. I suppose the story illustrated the importance of purity and obedience to God's laws, but all I could see was a rag-tag trail of tired mothers disappearing with pots and pans and wailing youngsters into the desert's horizon. I stood up. 'It wasn't their fault,' I shouted, and walked out.

In Berlin I asked Hermie about his leaving the Church. Did he miss it?

He replied that he still hadn't been able to feel the shocked liberation stage.

I laid my head on his chest. 'Was there comfort though?'

'Comfort in what?'

'In having that religious belief system?'

He sighed. 'I'm no longer waiting for salvation in an afterlife. But yes, there is comfort in the Sunday School delusion. The feeling that you are a child tucked into bed and listening to your parents milling around in the kitchen below.'

Arnaud walked me back to my *gîte* along a different route, where a dog charged a fence and a cat shot from a clump of wet lavender, a streak of marmalade orange.

'I despair you did not see the cherry tree in spring,' he said, his face wistful. 'It was magnificent. A tree like a poem.

So many flowers, as if it knew, as if it knew this was the last time.' He looked up at the damp evening sky. The rain had stopped but it was still misty enough. 'This weather. Finally, it is beginning to turn cooler. In Paris this summer the sky was bright pink all day long. No one cared. All that happened was more ice-cream vans came out for business. More vendors selling water in plastic bottles. The world is heating up. Like a war about to begin.'

I felt a wave of shame. Long-haul flights pour so much carbon into the atmosphere. All those people at Abu Dhabi where I'd changed planes, the sky shimmering outside, and I heard that earlier this year it shimmered just the same in Norway. No air-conditioning. People sticking together in buses. Too many travellers and me one of them. I need to stop moving but I can't, not yet.

'Still, we cannot be frozen with fear.' Arnaud interrupted my thoughts. 'We need to know the catastrophe is coming but we can't live in it every day. There is the fear and then the situation itself. We have to deny the fear sometimes or we would go crazy – *fou*,' he added in French. 'But then we must do something even if we do not know what to do or if it will work.'

It was when we stopped at my door that he told me about a tourist installation in Fismes. It follows the battle that destroyed the town. 'There were many writers among the soldiers,' he said. 'Pieces from their diaries are on display boards. They run along the Vesle River. The train station is nearby.' After he made a point of showing me how to secure the latch, he turned to leave and then turned back again. 'It is said World War I was the last poets' war. Yes, there is war but there is poetry too.'

Dearest, my mind is not in France in Sylvie's cottage at the beginning of autumn on a dark wet night. It is with you in Sydney in late summer. You are twenty-three years old and I have been back in Sydney for some seven years. We have been in closer contact; I've helped with school assignments and university applications. Lillian found out on one occasion and was cross – was that due to a slip of my tongue? You, in turn, were cross with me because you love Lillian and don't want her hurt – and because you and I are kindred spirits in writing and art and you didn't want that spoiled either.

On this particular day, we are in a brand-new flat, in a brand-new high rise, eleven stories up. The carpets are pink and the kitchen benches too high for you to use. The owner of the property has made it clear we are not to make any modifications for a disability. We aren't to leave a mark or a smudge.

I have placed a plastic runner at the door. Your wheelchair sits on that. Your body brace, the one you wear because, in consultation with Lillian, you declined to have a steel rod inserted in your back, is balanced against the wall. Your father has cut holes into the hard plastic to make it cooler to wear. He is not happy about you moving out of home, but you have told him the flat is part of a student welfare package because you need to live closer to the city campus.

The part about subsidised accommodation is not true. Jeff and I are paying for the flat, hoping government support will eventually kick in, and I am feeling victorious because now I can visit you whenever I like.

My friend George, smart-mouthed, woolly-haired, clever George, who invented some sort of fin for a surfboard, is in your bathroom unscrewing glass frames from the shower stall. He has attached thin tubes and lever-handled taps to a backing board. The idea is to connect the tubes to the existing taps and place the backing board on the floor. This will allow you to operate the shower on your hands and knees.

He stores the glass frames in your wardrobe to be reinstalled at inspection times, calls me a nervous Nellie because at one point it looked as if he might drop them, although I think he is nervous too. Your ability to live in the flat with a fellow student depends on you being able to use the shower by yourself, and you have been craving this freedom.

Your large purple painting – the one that reminds me of an underwater shoreline, dark plants and creatures in helmet shells – leans against a wall. Another of your paintings stands on the bookshelf. It is a portrait of your sister. She is your father and Lillian's child. The portrait looks a little like Lillian and a lot like you. They also have a shy-eyed son.

This means five siblings including Louis, whom I gave birth to five years after Max. A miraculous arrival again. But you, you are my only daughter, the one who shouts opinions across a university lecture hall and has earned a degree in visual arts. I have told everyone how theatre design was part of the course, but you went ahead and wrote a play as well. 'How hard can it be?' you said. You always say that and, encouraged by your lecturer, went on to apply for a place in the postgraduate program at the National Institute of Dramatic Art. The head of the interview panel asked, 'So why do you want to pursue a playwright career?'

You glanced down at the body brace and electric wheelchair. 'Have we got a lot of other options here?'

George is ready for you to test his adaptation, and you do that thing where you rest your palms on the floor and straighten your back legs like a newborn colt, shuffling on palms and feet towards the bathroom, where you drop back onto your knees. That crash. I wonder how often you can drop like that before your kneecaps snap, although medical specialists have been amazed at your ability to move. You wouldn't have been able to move like that with a rod in your back.

Now you are crawling forward, the mane of auburn hair, those impossibly thin and elegant arms. You hit a tap with your elbow and the water comes on. George leans against the tiled wall. His eyes fill with tears. You glance up. 'It's good plumbing, George, not diamonds that are a girl's best friend.'

Once George is finished with the plumbing, I paint Slipgard on the shower-room floor and set up the VitalCALL hardware. 'Your roommate needs to know how to use this too,' I say, testing the button.

You don't like it on the dressing table. Makes it feel like a hospital room. 'My roommate is just for back-up,' you reply. 'I can do most things myself.'

George has also jigged up a low table with an electrical cord so you can prepare meals at wheelchair height – me with the idea you would be spinning around the kitchen like one of those Paralympians. But you have refused to use it, instead getting around on your hands and knees. The microwave lies on your bedroom floor next to a loaf of bread and a tub of margarine. You've run over the margarine with your wheelchair, leaving a long greasy smear. When you go out, you roll inside your brace, then onto a low ottoman, and then onto your bed. From there you slide into your wheelchair and then fume when the special taxi you've booked is running late. It was often late that first term and later still when you were ready to return. You'd sit in front of the university buildings, dusk settling, and then call me. I'd want to throw you onto the back seat of my car, but you wouldn't leave the electric wheelchair behind, so we'd wait and wait. We talked about – what are we talking about? The sky above is inky, tin stars threaded on thin string. You spin the electric wheelchair around like a racing car driver. Nimble. You are nimble on your wheels.

Your father worried that you were not eating properly, but he always worries that people are not eating enough. When we were married, he'd hold out a sandwich, a cream bun, whatever was in his hand. 'Do you want a bite?' Even when I was in labour with you he appeared with a ham sandwich, offering it as I groaned through a contraction.

No, I didn't want to be fed, not then, and not now, but I was noticing and not noticing you becoming more fragile. You were my daughter who could not be a ballerina but would become everything else. You move your arm. Your scapulas jut from your back. I see them and look away.

'When was the last time you saw a specialist?' I ask.

You reply that you are in positive denial and I'm your co-conspirator until, until – until one dull summer morning your roommate calls to tell me you have pressed the VitalCALL button. An ambulance is on its way.

You have pneumonia. It is January. One year since you moved out. It will be April before you are released from hospital. You've lost the ability to sit up. The specialists tell us there is nothing more they can do.

Your father stands feverish beside your bed. He doesn't want to hear this. He wants you back inside your body brace, lifts you into the wheelchair, grasps your hand and forces it over the control buttons. But you can't breathe in the brace now, tumble forward. In the end, hospital orderlies transport you on a trolley, and once back inside your flat, we are eager for them to leave us alone. We believe – you believe too – that if we place you on the pink carpet you will be able to crawl again, do that crab walk to the toilet. Everything will return to the way it was before.

But it didn't.

Is this my fault? Should I have helped you move out? I still remember that moment when you said you didn't want to be the crippled girl in a room at the back of your father's house – and daylight, I am remembering the daylight in your hair as you lay on a blanket on the balcony of that brand-new flat with your friend, two city girls plotting the adventure ahead.

There is nothing ahead in the next scene, just constant now. Frangipani blooms and slices of apple decorate little shrines around the flat. Tibetan prayer flags flutter on the balcony. Your father has wrangled a way of putting the twin sisters of a friend on the carers' pension and topping up the amount to make it worthwhile. The twins are Buddhists. They have been covering three days and two nights a week. The rest of the family cover the other shifts. Since leaving the hospital you require 24-hour care.

The hospital trolley that brought you home is in the living room. We kept it because you were discharged without a commode, or a trolley we could tip in case we needed to pound phlegm out of your chest, or a suction machine in case you choked on your food. Lillian bought a suction machine at great expense and then snatched tubes from the hospital supply cupboard, some other things as well. I was impressed with this theft, the way she stuffed the packets in her bag.

Your father, Lillian, Jeff and I have entered détente after reaching the beyond of the beyond as we remain on high, high alert listening for your every breath, your every cough. Night shift means getting up to adjust your CPAP mask again and again and again. It doesn't fit. Nothing fits – no hoist, no mask, no toilet-chair height. You are bespoke – your back that dips into an impossible hollow because there is no steel rod holding it straight, your tiny face and the lips that can't seal. You've come up with ideas: raising your bed on bricks, placing a facewasher over your ears to fill out the chin strap, stuffing tissues into the plastic cap around your nose.

On this particular day you are resting in your room while the Buddhist twins, two social workers, Lillian, your father, a young man from the Community Options team and I crowd into the living room, although I can't see Jeff. Maybe he comes later.

Your father begins setting up an Italian espresso machine and placing pastries on plates. He wears a smart suit, in contrast to my ratty ponytail and crumpled polyester pants. While he puts on his show, I am putting on mine. I reckon for this scene a ragged soldier crawling out of a ditch is more appropriate. We need reinforcements, not a catering award. I'm also making a statement against Lillian, who is wearing a linen sheath and matching jacket: corporate person versus wrung-out mother. Wrung-out mothers cut it better with social workers. I'm vying for best mother and already winning; their sympathetic looks are aimed at me.

The Community Options guy asks everyone to sit in a circle. Lillian tells him how we are trying to look after you and hold down full-time jobs, and that her son is studying for his Higher School Certificate. She wants to make sure he gets good grades. As for her own house, her own house is upside down – at least, that's what comes out of her mouth. She doesn't have the language for this situation.

I say Louis has become withdrawn. He is eleven years old. When I asked him to tell me what was on his mind he replied, 'It's too small. There are too many bigger things than me.' As for Max, he's running wild. Higher School Certificate. Fat chance.

I see the young man from Community Options calculate these casualties. 'I've heard enough,' he says, rising from a cushion on the floor. 'We'll raid several funding sources. We'll get you more support and nine days respite leave. We're going to give you back your life.'

'Go to China,' you said, when I came into your room afterwards. 'Go mental. If I could get out of here I'd go mental too. Stop in Hong Kong on the way. Have a suit made, a tailor-made suit to last your whole life. I'll design it and borrow it when you return.'

Nine whole days. A whole life. The idea of it was like stepping inside a snow globe. You and me boarding the miniature train that winds up a mountain peak. The scene grows large and full around us both, so that I can see you sitting opposite on the leather seat wearing a felt hat with a slanted brim. You designed the hat too.

But it wasn't us clacking up a snow peaked mountain, was it. And Hong Kong didn't feel like China, more like Westfield Shopping Mall in Penrith. I showed your design to a tailor in one of the narrow shops, while he was measuring Jeff for several shirts. He was impressed with your drawings, but shook his head. 'I don't stock fabrics that would drape like that.'

No, the China you told me to visit didn't come until we flew to Guilin in the middle of the night. It felt as if I'd been dropped into the aftermath of a war there too. Vehicles packed the dark highway as if fleeing occupied territory, our taxi jostling between scooters, trucks and bicycles, faces lit with headlights and then gone. One small truck had a whole family squeezed into what looked like a wooden cage on the back. A little girl with a moon face like yours peered out. Jeff and I were the rich Westerners headed for the faded opulence of a grand hotel.

Jeff fell into a deep sleep immediately after we checked into our room, but I lay awake listening to ballroom music in a thin cat-yowl pitch. I drew back the curtain to see the grainy shadows of people waltzing on the footpath below. It was early dawn, spring in China, the countryside covered in fog. Children materialised out of the thick mist selling roses. Hawkers called out *hello, hello* when we finally ventured outside. A man appeared among them to enquire in very fine English if we were lost. He wore a jacket and tie. Jeff thought he might be from the nearby university, and when he offered to show us the sights we happily went along. But he took us to shop stands where we were supposed to buy a painting, or a sculpture, or an antique magnifying glass. I felt duped, until you, who were not there but were there, told me to buy the magnifying glass.

'The shops give him a commission,' you whispered. 'Look at the pockets of his suit; they are threadbare. There are children at home.'

I still have the magnifying glass. The handle is jade. An intricate metal decoration holds the glass. And now I am remembering how we bought Louis a second-hand piano and a puppy before leaving for China. The puppy because it was so careless and loveable, quite stupid too. We had to rush it to the vet because it had eaten something in the park, vomited up a used condom, blue plastic tubing and the remnants of a hotdog, green and probably eight days old. As for the piano, I hoped Louis might take lessons and because pianos – the wood, the ivory – are beautiful in themselves.

The piano was delivered a few days before we were due to fly and I discovered some of the keys were broken. Touch them and they didn't make a sound. On that day, I also received a call from the hospital, or perhaps more specifically from researchers connected to the hospital, asking for blood samples from me and my parents in Canada. They made the same request of your father, his parents too. Genetic testing had advanced considerably since you were first diagnosed. There was a possibility your condition was not a spontaneous mutation. The disease could express itself in various ways. Symptoms in other family members could be mild, almost imperceptible. Perhaps nothing more than a weak, flat smile.

The request for blood testing felt like a strange victory, a rare moment where I was being recognised as your mother. I was also betting the genetic mutation would be on your father's side. Something had to be that side's fault. Your father is the one with the flat smile. Whereas my smile is radiant. I show all of my teeth.

We returned from China to discover the puppy had dug a large hole in the backyard and chewed the floor-length curtains to shreds. I'd asked a friend to stay with Max and Louis while we were away but agreed she could leave a day early. It was safe enough to have a sixteen-year-old in charge of an eleven-year-old and a puppy for one night. But there had been a party: rap dancing, bongs and beer. I was on my hands and knees polishing scratches out of the wood floor when the telephone rang. The results of the blood tests had come in.

Facioscapulohumeral muscular dystrophy. What a mouthful. First the face. Then the shoulders. Then the limbs. But not everyone progresses that way. I think it was a female voice that relayed how the condition was the result of deletions on a particular chromosome. The lab had mapped something like ninety deletions in you, while I had forty-nine. I think she said forty-nine, but remember, I'm not good with numbers. I'm not good with maps. It's story lines that are my strength, and the story I heard was this: the mutation occurred at my mother's conception, not in her chromosomes, but in her eggs, of which I was one. Among some of my own eggs there was further mutation, and one of them was you. The lab assistant added that genes mutated all of the time and then said something about low-level genetic instability in germ line cells being critical to the evolutionary process because the instability generates variability within species that supports population adaptation to selective pressures.

I put down the phone, moved to press one of those silent keys on the piano and then retrieved the Chinese magnifying glass from the suitcase I hadn't unpacked, the one you had told me to buy. I recalled a friend telling me that from time to time I looked older. This was when I was nineteen and wanted to look older. 'When I have my hair up?' I'd asked.

'No, just from certain angles.'

I took out the family albums. My father once told me if you place your hand over one side of a portrait you can see both sides of a person's character. And there it was under the magnifying glass, photos of me where one side of my face appeared slightly surprised and lost, and the other ready for battle. A grimace. Half of a flat smile that had progressed over the years.

Facioscapulohumeral muscular dystrophy is asymmetrical. I am weaker on my right, ever so slightly; you are weaker on your left. I'd been so ready to blame your father. The genetic mutation started with me. Wonky genes. It felt like a moral defect, as if I was lacking in morality and your body carried the shame. But upon hearing the news, you said, 'I like being mutable! I like the idea we can change into something else!' The disease bound us together: you, me, my mother – all of us strung together along a threaded line.

'Now find my brother!' You bumped my arm with your hand, a floppy slap because your wrist was so weak.

Did I thank you properly for that? How you saw through me? How you knew he'd never left my heart, that children never do. How I'd marked his birthday silently as much as I'd marked yours and your brothers. May in Canada. The time of tulips, spring and skipping ropes.

I don't think I said anything to you at the time – well, you were only seven when countries around the world began overturning laws governing adoption agreements. I read reunion registers were being opened in Australia and that Ontario had opened one too. I applied right away even though nothing could happen until your brother turned eighteen. Later, when visiting my parents to introduce them to one-year-old Max, I went to the registry in person, wanting to back up forms with an actual face. I also felt ridiculously hopeful that just by going to that building, walking up the steps, I would send a shiver through the universe that my son might feel, and at eighteen register his name too.

'It isn't as common for boys to go looking for their birth mothers,' the social worker said. 'And if they do, it's much later in life.'

I mentioned I had a daughter with muscular dystrophy, hoped that information might shake something, then felt guilty using you.

'Use me again!' you shouted, hearing the whole of the story the day the genetic results came back.

Of course, you know the rest of the story, but it is lovely to speak it once more because in terms of the timing it is improbable and filled with a strange kind of wonder like you. We contacted the research team. They were aghast, felt all this secrecy and waiting for an approach by the affected party was the most ridiculous thing they'd ever heard. A letter was sent to the Adoption Registry in Ontario, and the same day it arrived on their desk – well, maybe it wasn't exactly the same day, but it makes a better story – your eldest half-brother walked in. At first he was told it would take months and months to check files for a match, but there was the letter. The social worker was staggered too.

That May I flew back through seasons and time into a Canadian spring, and was whooshed into the body of the teenager that I had been then. Spring is such a miracle in Canada, the great melting and then the sun on dry cement. My shoes made a click, click on the sidewalk as I swung up the steps of my son's apartment. When his eyes met mine, he gasped lightly, as if fogging a mirror before wiping it clean.

'I've never been in a room with anyone who looked like me before,' he said, his eyes so familiar, the long slim fingers like yours, although he does not have this disease.

Who suffers most from this weakening condition? Who supports whom? I took you on that trip to Scotland with your aunt Alice when you were nineteen because I'd travelled at that age. I also wanted to put my mothering abilities on display: carrying you up flights of stairs into an aircraft, assembling wheelchairs, lowering you into baths. Do you remember the wooden footrest we had made so you could balance on the airline seat, except it kept sliding back and forth so you couldn't balance, and within no time were in such pain? Eventually, I held you on my lap, a young woman who was taller than me, you twisting and turning trying to get comfortable as I tried to gather up your long limbs.

You asked to be taken to the toilet over and over again, and I carried you there too. Passengers whispered and stared. On the last trip, you told me to leave you in the toilet alone, but it was too dangerous.

'Then turn around!' You were so tired of people staring.

I turned and leaned against the wall, my jaw tight from holding back tears. You asked if I was crying.

'No.'

'Yes, you are. Your shoulders are shaking.' You were right, tears were falling too. I heaved for a while and then you said, 'Let's stay in here forever.' And when I turned my wet face around, you started to laugh, and then I began laughing hard too, doubling over and close to throwing up.

We stayed in the toilet cubicle for almost an hour, and later, when we were waiting in the airport for our next connection, you told me to stretch out over a plastic bench and kept an eye on the clock as I slept.

Sometimes I dream this disease backward. You are lying across the modified wheelchair and then you are back in your brace sitting up in your regular electric wheelchair, and then you are simply holding on to the handles of a push wheelchair to balance as you walk. And then I am in the wheelchair, and you are pushing me.

Marne Region,
north-eastern France
1 October 2017

Sylvie appeared in the backyard this morning to prepare the *gîte* next door for new guests. She was shaking out rugs. The red kerchief tied around her hair stood up in the breeze like a small flag. She caught sight of me in the window, waved, then soon after arrived at the front door carrying a cutting board and teapot. She explained that before I came, a large family had taken over both sides of the cottage. Several things ended up in the wrong kitchen as a result. She wanted to make sure nothing else was missing. Could she come in? Was I going out?

'No,' I replied, as much to the question of her coming in as the possibility of me going out. I didn't want her to see me and the kitchen looking such a mess, stale baguette crumbs all over the table and four cups of cold tea I hadn't tipped out. I followed her around as she peered in cupboards and cutlery drawers, trying to distract her by saying how very grateful I was for the teapot. I'd been making tea in the coffee press, as if this explained the dirty cups.

She turned. 'But you should ask when you need something,' she said, noticing I hadn't switched on the heating panels and bending to turn on one near the door. 'I think you are the *stoïque*. You do not expect the life to be kind around you, but you are in France now. You should eat nice things. Drink champagne.'

I replied I was from Scotland originally and so used to the cold, although I didn't mind, I didn't mind at all her turning the heating on. It was just that I hadn't noticed.

'The research,' she said glancing at the mess on the table. 'It takes all the space in your head? I hope you are not disturbed when people stay next door, but soon there will be no one coming with summer gone. So, you can be the hermit. But do go out from time to time.'

'I did go out yesterday,' I replied. I didn't want her to know that I find it difficult to do anything more than stare out the attic window or come downstairs in my pyjamas to scribble notes to you. I did the same on the island in the Outer Hebrides. Braved distance and winter storms to get there and then had spells where all I could do was listen to the wind wail and watch re-runs of *Mary Poppins* and *Nanny McPhee*. How you loved those films as a little girl.

'And I'm not a hermit,' I added, trying to sound light as I began tidying up the mess on the table. I was messy in Berlin too. Hermie used to call me the civilian, someone who didn't put anything away. He strutted like a soldier at times, barked opinions that sounded like orders in a way that woke me up. I need waking up.

'My friend has been held up in America,' I added, to prove that I did hang out with people and because it seemed to open the possibility that Hermie might appear. I felt my face burn red at the thought, and wanting to change the subject I said I was going to Fismes later to see the Writers Walk.

Sylvie frowned. 'The what? I've never heard of this thing.'

I was slightly annoyed then at the red scarf around her head, and the authority in her voice that suggested if she hadn't heard of the walk then it didn't exist.

After she left, I showered and dressed, intent on bringing back evidence. I also found myself happy to be in the car again, my muddy, scratched partner in crime. This time I found my way to Fismes easily enough but on approaching the town entered a traffic circle on the left and almost collided with another driver entering from the right. He began waving his arms, shouting in French. I rolled down the window trying to explain how I was used to driving on the other side of the road. Three drivers backed up behind him and began waving their arms as well, although everyone was very polite once they understood my mistake, all of them reversing as best they could and pointing in the direction I was meant to go.

But let me tell you what happened in Fismes. First, I will describe the town, which has rows of chalky brick houses decorated with wooden window shutters and curlicue wrought iron on the rooftops that look like lacy hats. The

Town Hall resembles a toy castle, turrets and flags flapping gaily. There is a paved square lined with shops, and a police station nearby. After the incident in the traffic circle I thought it best to find the Writers Walk on foot and parked on the side of the square. But as I got out, the car began rolling forward. I'd forgotten the handbrake, and given there was a small incline, it crashed into the back step of a van parked in front. I tried to push it back but immediately policemen came running like the gendarmes in a Tintin comic book. '*Éloignez-vous!*' they shouted, and began snapping photographs from every angle. I wasn't to touch anything until the van driver returned. He eventually emerged from a shop, a small, neatly built man with large, hooded eyes. '*Merde*,' he muttered when he realised the commotion involved him. With his help, my car was finally pushed back to reveal a smashed grill and a small black box dangling on two wires. It turned out to be the sensor. I couldn't see much damage to the van's back step, but still more photos were taken, and notes written down.

    The police asked for my insurance details, which I'd left in the cottage, and flustered beyond belief, I babbled in broken French how I could go back to the cottage and get the insurance forms, and then told the van driver where the cottage was, and how Sylvie was my host, and how I could leave my wallet with him if that was any help. I don't think he understood a word. One of the policemen raced back to the station and dragged out a colleague who spoke English. He was able to clarify the situation for the driver and added that if we wanted to settle it between ourselves it was fine with the police, given both vehicles were safe to drive. It turned out the van had a broken sensor too, the one that lowered and raised the back step.

The driver, whom I will call Philippe (he looked like a Philippe), said he trusted me and would come later in the afternoon. I gave him clear instructions to knock on the smaller door of the cottage and then wandered off aimlessly, not quite remembering why I was in Fismes in the first place, and certainly not game to get back in the car. It was during this wandering that I saw the train station in the distance and a river with a stone bridge above. Of course, the Writers Walk. But despite crossing from one side of the bridge to the other and peering over the low wall to the riverbank below, I saw no sign of a display, only sandstone pillars at one end honouring the 28th Division of American Soldiers who'd fought with the French. Further away, men sat on stools outside a café drinking wine in the late morning sun. One looked old enough to have seen out a war so I approached and asked if he knew of the installation. '*Bonjour. Savez-vous les tableaux d'affichage de la guerre?*'

I could tell right away he did not like the look of me. He turned to a young man in a black apron who was stacking glasses. '*Tu lui parles,*' he said. You speak to her.

I expected the young man to ignore me too, but his face lit up. '*Oui, les Américains! Le monument est sur l'autre côté du pont.*' He took my arm and led me back to the sandstone pillars. '*L'ecriture. La guerre,*' he said, pointing to the inscriptions carved on each base and then at the soldiers faces carved at the top. '*Les soldats!*'

I thanked him, pretending the pillars were what I'd been hoping to find, and when he was well on his way back to the café, I continued down the road hoping to run into one of the display boards further on. As I walked I began thinking of Hermie again, something about those carved military faces and the monument being erected by the State of Pennsylvania – not that Hermie is from Pennsylvania, but he'd once told me that when he was a boy he'd painted the flags belonging to everyone who'd come to America on the side of his parents' garage, even the Vikings. He wanted to honour them all – and I was thinking of the small boy he'd been and the earnest belief in a particular kind of bravery and goodness that stood straight and tall. I had the same sort of fervour when I was a kid singing in the church choir in Canada and wondering if, like Jesus, I could take nails being hammered into my hands and feet. Don't laugh. I can hear you laughing already.

During that summer and into the early autumn I'd get up early each morning and walk the cliff edge above Lake Ontario hoping to catch the pure moment between the dawn breaking and the first sin of the day. Turn right and there was The Waterworks, an imposing treatment plant inside an opulent 1930s art deco building of marble entryways and vast halls filled with pools of water and filtration equipment that still services almost half of Toronto and beyond. We called it the Waterworks but in earlier years it earned the nickname The Palace of Purification. I usually turned left, away from the building, into parkland, but this particular morning was drawn to turn right. It was mid-September. I had just turned ten and was wearing a ring my parents had given me for my birthday that I loved with all my heart. As I walked I came across three utility poles standing in a stretch of grass. Who knows why they were there without any wires and not connected to anything else. But I imagined they were the crosses on Calvary Hill appearing to raise the question:

Hey, little girl, are you brave enough to have nails hammered into your flesh?

Given I couldn't show devotion by being nailed to a cross, I took off my birthday ring and laid it in the grass. It was the best sacrifice I could make, just like I came to believe later that the best sacrifice I could make was to hand over my first child. The Anglican novice in the home for unwed mothers told us Moses' mother loved her child enough to let him go. And with Christopher and you – well, there was that other biblical scene in King Solomon's Court. When faced with passing judgment on two women who were arguing over the ownership of a child, King Solomon recommended the infant be sliced in two and each given half. It was the birth mother who shook her head frantically and cried, 'No, give the baby to her.'

I think in the end King Solomon declared her to be the real mother. But that was a story; it never happened to me.

I was thinking these things as I walked further and further down the road in Fismes, until the footpath fell away and I found myself walking through long grass at the side of an open road. I spotted a plot of thin trees in the distance that reminded me of the utility poles I'd seen as a kid. I turned onto a grassy swale to approach them, stepping through marshy ground. It felt as if I was following my ten-year-old self, although this time I wasn't imagining I was walking up Calvary Hill towards Jesus hanging on a cross, I was imagining this was where I'd find Section E.

Sunlight streaked through the slim trees in a way that resembled the narrow aisles of a church, and as I grew closer my feet began sinking deeper and deeper into mud. This was a bog. I was walking into a bog. Someone shouted from the road. *Arrêtez! Que faites-vous? Sortez d'ici!'*

Philippe arrived at Sylvie's cottage to find me trying to clean my shoes. He was carrying his insurance papers, two spots on his cheeks glowing pink because I think he was embarrassed to be alone with me. I was embarrassed too. I could smell the light sweat on his shirt and was close enough to see a nick where he'd shaved. He stood next to the kitchen table and launched into a complicated legal explanation in French. My vocabulary doesn't extend to vehicle parts, so I suggested we use my laptop's translation program. The laptop was on the table beside the letters I've been writing to you. I demonstrated how he could type into the translation square in French and that it would appear in English in the box opposite. Philippe spent some time starting sentences and deleting words, but I came to understand he didn't want to claim on his insurance. He'd been to his garage and the cost of replacing the sensor was one hundred and fifty euros, whereas he could buy the sensor for fifty euros and replace it himself with no effect on his premium. If I gave him the money we'd be square.

I was happy to give him fifty euros but didn't have it on me at the time. I also wanted to fill in my insurance form regardless, as I would need to submit a claim for the damaged rental car. We were sorting out a time to meet again when he began to stutter, 'My English is...' He shook his head. 'I have the sister who speaks English.'

Why was he telling me this? Did he want to consult his sister? Did he want to bring her with him just to make sure? Without waiting for me to respond he pointed at the confusion on the kitchen table. 'What is these things? Why are you in France?' It was as if he thought something sinister was going on.

'*Je fais des recherches sur l'histoire de la Grande Guerre,*' I began in my awful, halting French, but then had the ghastly feeling I was going to burst into tears. I glanced at the laptop, remembering a Chinese writer once telling me that she couldn't write her story in Chinese, but she could in English. The language separated her from the events as if they had happened to someone else. I leaned over the laptop ready to begin but considered Philippe might frame the information in a particular way. I won't have you framed. So I began typing that I was writing about a war over asparagus, a war about the benefits of food. And then I looked at him fiercely – at least, I thought my expression was fierce.

In those mythic days, when we were fierce, you figured out a way of lowering the wheelchair backrest and turning the armrests and controls around so you could lie over the seat and drive prone. Lulu became your guard-dog in a rhinestone collar perched on the front. I was the outrider at your side. We conversed loudly about Erté and Chagall, and anything else erudite. We laughed, a force field to combat sympathetic stares.

I bought Lulu against Lillian's wishes, against the Buddhist twins' wishes, against the rules of the corporate body managing the building. I was remembering myself as a girl in a basement apartment in Canada. No dogs allowed there either and me telling my mother I didn't want anything for Christmas because the one thing I wanted so badly I couldn't have. 'Fair enough,' she replied, and left me to sulk.

Strangely, two weeks before Christmas, she announced guests were coming for dinner – strange because we never had people for dinner. It was such a small apartment, no dining room; we were hard-pressed to squeeze around the kitchen table ourselves. Small windows looked up on car wheels in a parking lot above our heads. The plumbing leaked; part of the ceiling had come down. My father stuffed some red long johns into the hole to make it look as if Santa Claus was falling through the roof.

That evening, my mother called me into the kitchen to introduce me to a smart young couple in winter coats. At their feet was a wall-eyed spaniel puppy. I thought it was their puppy and asked if I could pat it, but as I kneeled my mother said, 'Happy Christmas. He's yours.' Even now my heart breaks with the joy. This puppy, the runt of a litter, one blue eye, one brown, that my parents were able to get cheap and my father trained not to bark. We would have been evicted from the apartment if the puppy made a peep.

Lulu was the runt of her litter too. I will always hold the memory of carrying her to your bedroom and asking you to close your eyes and open your arms. You brought your head down to her warm body while she licked tears from your face. Do you remember how we smuggled her in and out of the building in a large handbag slung over my arm, her little face looking up from the bottom waiting for the moment when we told her it was okay to come out? Those were the days when you wore a blue scarf and black gloves, cool days when the leaves on the plane trees turned brown and blew over the streets and stuck to windows in the rain. The days when we bought ginger and chocolate from a Victorian arcade in the city. A new foundation was raising funds to research your disease and had asked if they could put your artwork on greeting cards. In Balmain, a gallery had accepted your etchings, with no inkling you had a disability. They gaped when you rolled in.

'You never mentioned…'

'But you like my art…' you replied.

That day you had manoeuvred the wheelchair through crowded city streets, gridlocked crossings. The light turned green. People snaked through the cars but there was no room for you. We were trapped behind a young man in a cardigan. Your electric wheelchair bumped the kerb. He turned, saw your face down there and Lulu's nose, and suddenly he was banging on the hoods of cars, shouting at the drivers to back up. 'See what you have done!' he screamed as if they had put you in the wheelchair, caused this disease. Inch by inch the cars backed up.

People told us you were lucky you weren't in a nursing home, lucky, lucky that professional carers filled in shifts and were able to take you out. How did you avoid a nursing home?

I wanted to paint on the side of skyscrapers that it cost more to keep people in nursing homes than pay carers. Oh, the look on the faces of the women from the government department who wanted to cut your budget, wanted you off their books. They arrived at the door, one dressed in a cream skirt and carrying a folder with a green adhesive label. What did green mean? The other one stood slightly hunched as if she didn't want to be there, kept glancing nervously at the artwork in the corridor. Maybe it made the entrance look too fancy. Lucky, lucky us.

The one with the folder was so eager to tell me how much your care was costing, the most expensive case on her books. Seated at your table, she opened the folder while I whispered to the other woman that those were your paintings on the walls. A gallery in Balmain had agreed to take you on. I told her about the research foundation too, how wonderful it was your carers were able to take you to meetings when I was at work.

At that moment, a carer, the one with the lovely long hair and Bali T-shirts, wheeled you out of your room. The woman with the folder didn't look up. She was still leafing through pages, still reinforcing how they needed to cut back. 'We can replace her long-term carers with casuals. Casuals can drop in for a couple of hours to give her a shower and cook her food, but they can't take her out. Can she feed herself?'

I turned to you. 'Can you feed yourself?'

The room was filled with thick silence as the woman with the folder finally looked up. It's always a shock. You on your stomach, those impossibly thin arms. Her offsider leaned in. 'She's an artist. She makes greeting cards for a research foundation. She has a gallery exhibition opening soon.'

'But of course,' I butted in, 'this would be very difficult to maintain without support.'

I shouldn't have needed to do this. I shouldn't have needed to turn you into a super cripple – a word you used and have often said you never wanted to be. Remember the young man from Community Options saying it didn't matter what a person with a disability does; they shouldn't need to prove themselves as being the sort of person who is harnessing the moon to get appropriate care? Yet I was playing this card, even as the woman with the folder was insinuating you were eating someone else's breakfast. The real issue was the need for a larger pie, not a lot of people fighting for a tiny slice.

'I suppose you are very proud of your daughter,' she said, as if this was a fault. 'I suppose you would be upset if her achievements were compromised in any way.'

I'm not sure what she was going to say next – her mouth was open for it – perhaps she was going to tell me something about how we all have to make sacrifices, but she was interrupted.

'I feel uncomfortable with this,' said her offsider, clearly distressed. 'If she can't continue with her gallery show and the research foundation – well, it's the sort of story you might see on *A Current Affair*.'

I leaned forward. 'Oh, you can count on it.'

I said this with the same tone and sweet smile that Lillian uses when she hates someone. She's used it on me. It's a tone that implies she's offering another ribbon sandwich, perhaps a fresh serviette.

They left. We received a letter that your arrangements wouldn't be tampered with again. But that was us. Not everyone else. I think of the young man in the manual wheelchair at the entrance of the hospital during the period when you had been in intensive care with pneumonia and were told to spend a little time in the sunlight. You wore pink leggings, a pink jacket and matching sunglasses to be among a huddle of people wearing hospital gowns. Some were hooked up to plastic bags on portable metal poles, and that young man – I remember him so clearly, his bare feet like round heads of radicchio, purple streaked, his stained track suit pants and torn flannel shirt – he kept taking sidelong glances at you, eventually flicked the butt of his cigarette, guided his wheelchair forward. 'What's wrong with you?' He took in the trolley you were on. The jacket disguised your thin arms. You liked to pretend you were a movie star who'd met with a skiing accident.

'Not much.'

He lit another cigarette, took in the full length of you again. 'Pressure ulcers for me this time,' he said. 'The group-home is understaffed, but better than a nursing home.' He glanced at me, and I felt in his expression again the warning that one must wear the hangdog face and torn shirt to get support. My mind flickered to the period not long after you were born. Your father and I were behind in rent and I was making every penny stretch and stretch. I was terribly thin then too. Kept thinking of the things I didn't need to eat. The local doctor sent a social worker to my door. She wanted to run through a budget, clicked her tongue when she heard I'd spent scarce resources on saving a front tooth.

'That was extravagant. You should have had the dentist pull it out.'

And so it would have begun. The gap. The bogan grin. Easily identified. Those people. Why are people in strife expected to dress down, have bad haircuts and bad teeth? When your CPAP mask began pushing in your front teeth I banged on doors until I found a dental specialist willing to make an orthodontic plate. 'Braces?' A friend asked. 'You were worried about the look of her teeth with everything else going on?'

Yes, I worried about teeth, because my father had worried about teeth. He said if you can get yourself a suit and a decent smile no one had to know where you'd come from, so we'd had braces instead of decent furniture, although perhaps with you I was only decorating the trenches with tinsel, pretending you and I were never even close to the Front.

I'm not fierce now. Simply reckless. In Berlin I followed directions along a dimly lit road in cold November to a railway overpass, steel railings sparkling with frost and a signpost pointing in three directions like a broken weathervane waiting for the wind to blow. In the Outer Hebrides I walked in blinding rain across a beach that also served as a landing strip when the tide went out. Windsocks were blowing, the traffic controller shouting, 'Can you no read the danger sign! A plane's about to land!'

No, I can't read danger signs. Or is it that I don't want anyone telling me the nature of danger anymore, the nature of risk? I have too long imagined myself in your body and the minds of others, unable to read the churnings of my own stomach and heart. I need to feel the rain strike my face, see the shadow of a plane with my own eyes, and run if I must, because the muscles in my own legs fire and tell me to run.

That day on the tiny island in the Outer Hebrides while the traffic controller was shouting, a car pulled over on the roadside above the beach. A man stuck his face out of the window, called out, 'D'ya need a lift?' I clambered up the bank and climbed into the passenger seat sopping wet. The driver wore a bulky overcoat and turned to look at me with watery blue island eyes, then quickly back at the windscreen. He was one of those people who let you be.

'I'm headed to Castle Bay,' he said, and left it at that. The rain came in heavy. After a little while we approached a fork on the road. He slowed. 'Have you seen Vatersay Island?'

I turned to take in his round, chapped face.

He pointed to the right. 'It's just across the causeway. Land of Freedom, home of the Vatersay Raiders who built huts and planted potatoes on Lady Gordon of Cathcart's property and landed themselves in Edinburgh jail.' His face suddenly split with a grin. 'I'm a descendant you know. Fierce wild men are we. The trip will only take you a wee while.'

I shrugged.

The fork took us across the causeway and the road rose up a steep ridge that bordered a cliff overlooking slippery grey rocks and web-footed seals. My companion pointed out an empty cottage where a woman, apparently holidaying from abroad, once shut herself away. 'Told her family back home that she was fine and then disappeared, a bag of potatoes on the table, dishes in the sink...' He trailed off, leaving the story there, and didn't speak again until we reached a small, white church on a steeper rise. Its drystone wall surrounded a patch of scrubby grass. The church roof was dull blue tile.

'Our Lady of the Waves,' he said, pulling up and asking if I wanted to go in, which I did because I needed to be away from the noise of the hammering rain.

It was quiet inside: simple wood pews, votive candles on a side table, and to the right of the altar a doll's house, or at least my memory conjures up a doll's house surrounded with Christmas lights, large acorn-shaped ones, and nativity figurines within.

My new acquaintance asked if I wanted to stay in the church for a little while, and that he could wait outside the door. But before he left, he stuffed a five-pound note in the votive candle box and struck a match.

'This is for you,' he said, lighting one candle. Then as he lit two more: 'And this one for whoever you're grieving over, and the last one here for the rest of your team.'

Who was my team? The candles flickered. There was the sulphur odour of the burnt matchhead. There was the softening wax and honest wood floor.

By the time I came out the rain had cleared. Early twilight was settling. The driver was leaning on the drystone wall picking his nails. Once we were back in the car, he asked if I'd like to go down to one of the coves while there was still light. I nodded and we drove down a hill to where the road stopped at a wire fence. He got out, showed me how to climb over the wire, past a few cows, and then down a grassy slope to a tiny curved beach. Salt-white sand. He rolled up his trousers, pulled off his shoes and socks. 'D'ya want to go for a paddle?' he asked. And when I looked startled, 'C'mon, it's the middle of winter. The Atlantic Ocean. It'll be fuckin' freezing.'

I was reminded of the time my father found me fretting over final high school exams. He had little understanding of the Canadian schooling system, little understanding of the course material either, having left school himself at fourteen. That wintry afternoon he drove me down to Lake Ontario, marched me across the snowy beach, and dared me to run three times around a tyre floating in the colder than cold waves beyond. And I did. He did too. Both of us screaming, then back inside his truck, our feet and legs green with cold. He turned on the heater, took his packet of Sweet Virginia tobacco out of his pocket and filled his pipe. 'Now,' he said, after taking the first puff, 'all that terror has found an outlet. You can settle down, read those books.'

On Vatersay Island I splashed into the fuckin' freezing Atlantic Ocean and ran around in three big circles while the man with the watery blue eyes waited ankle deep in the shallows for me to be done. When I came out, he said the trick was to put on your socks and shoes while your feet were still wet. 'The sand will stick to them and give you a wee massage.'

He left me there on the beach for a while too, waited up near the wire fence with the cows. Then he drove me to his own croft, which was on the island, and put fresh mussels in a steaming pot. The sky outside was black by then and the small candlelit kitchen felt like the whole world. One last glowing ember of light. 'Aye,' he said. 'You looked like a lassie who needed a run in the Atlantic Ocean and a few candles lit.' Then he drove me home.

Marne Region,
north-eastern France
2 October 2017

Dearest girl, do you remember when Louis was old enough to take you to the pub? Louis, all long and gangly, trying to move chairs to allow your wheelchair past, and the guy in the corner table well into his cups who saw you and began blubbering, 'Oh Jesus, darling. Oh Jesus.' He pulled out his wallet. 'Here, let me give you something,' handing out five-dollar notes. Louis told him to put the money away but you slapped his arm.

'Take it. Take it. We'll buy some hot chips. It will make him feel better. It will make us feel better too.'

I am remembering this because Philippe arrived this morning to collect the fifty euros and then asked in faltering

English if he might come back again, just to visit. He said he felt sad for me and would like to help. It was beginning to rain by then as if the sky was wringing out dirty dishwater and the kitchen suddenly so grim and small. I couldn't bear his woeful eyes, and regretted I'd revealed anything of myself. I don't want kindness and I don't want continuities. Hermie isn't kind and there is no continuity with him. There is the Hermie in Berlin. There is the later Hermie who told me that he didn't believe in love anymore. There is the angry Hermie who isn't forgiving me for coming to France without him – the minister who preached forgiveness and can't offer forgiveness, the man with all of those military hats on hooks. I can't thread Hermie together into a story with meaning. He is just scenes. I feel him like broken waves on a morning swim. I used to go swimming in the early morning when you had pneumonia and couldn't breathe, and I couldn't breathe. I was living in that rental near Coogee Beach then, the place where the stupid puppy ate the curtains and Max had the hip-hop party. I swam through late summer, autumn and into the winter too, the water so cold it made me gulp for air. Hermie is like that. He hurts so much he makes me gulp for air.

I couldn't explain such things to Philippe. I lied and told him I was leaving the cottage and so it would be impossible to see him again. Some unreadable emotion crossed his face. He shrugged, said *au revoir* quickly and left without turning back. I felt bad listening to his van drive away, but I couldn't make him feel better. As he disappeared, Arnaud arrived, dashing across from his car.

'An accident,' I explained, standing at the door, because he would have seen Philippe driving away. 'I crashed into his van, but we're sorted now.'

'When?'

'When I went to Fismes to see the Writers Walk, but it doesn't appear to be there. Perhaps it has been taken down.'

'Perhaps you did not want to see it,' he replied jokingly, but narrowing his eyes in a way that suggested I'd avoided his poetry lesson, then pulling a large iron key from his pocket he announced, *'La clé de la cathédrale!'*

'The key to the cathedral?' I asked, confused, then realised he meant the one in Courville. 'Will Carole come too?'

'Ah, I think she would like me from under her feet and she is so keen that you see it. She does not think you have seen enough. She wants your research report to be very accurate, very successful. A report that will include our famous washhouses.' He laughed. 'You must take lots of photos and put them in your report.'

The village was not far away. Its streets were still wet from the drenching last night. We sloshed our way past trenches dug for the new sewer line. Arnaud pointed out the washhouse in the centre of the village. You would have laughed. Talk about grand. This one is brick with a hulking American eagle towering over its roof. The cathedral stood further up the hill, ghostly pale.

'It is made of chalkstone,' Arnaud said, as we tramped up the path. He unlocked the heavy door. Fossilised sea creatures were embedded in the front steps. I've woken from dreams where I've found the fossil remains of children in drawers, caught in layers of cardigans, handkerchiefs and underpants.

The light inside the church was soft and blotted. It wouldn't hurt your eyes and you would have liked the carvings of animal heads and fish. I thought of your purple painting, the underwater shore, and crossed myself at the altar. To the right a winding turret led to a gallery where wooden benches held broken pottery, stones and bits of glass. Arnaud guessed the collection was part of an archaeological dig, now abandoned. I was tempted to put something in my pocket, but felt you say no, leave everything as it was.

A second turret led to the chapel above, the one that connected to the now missing castle. It was a long, open room with wood scaffolding and the sound of pigeons fluttering, although I saw none of the birds about. Arnaud pointed out the cracked stone basin where archbishops once washed their hands and then to the fading remains of brick-red paint on the window recesses, a curvilinear pattern. But I hardly took it in. My eyes were darting around the room. Arnaud grew quiet. I had the sense he felt he was not being as useful as Carole in providing commentary. He asked again about my research. He didn't quite understand the nature of my project. *'Quels autres choses tu veux voir?* What other things do you need to see?'

I turned then, and finally confessed that I didn't know what I was looking for – only a connection between random things, and that I didn't even know what those random things were until I saw them.

He took hold of my shoulders and turned me to face the far end of the chapel. The clouds and rain outside were casting a misty glow over the chalkstone walls, pastel shades of rose, blue and green, yet the sky turning thunderous again outside. 'There, there,' he pointed. 'Take a photo of that.'

I did, then turned and stumbled down the narrow stairwell.

As we drove back, I felt I owed him some sort of explanation and so told him about the Catalan fairytale, about the brothers looking for the Water of Life and turning into stone and then mentioned the American eagle, how it was made out of stone and all the goddamn monuments, the triumphalism, the heroes. 'I am sick to death of heroes,' I suddenly shouted, thinking of you, thinking of myself.

'But we were inside a church,' he replied.

'Oh, churches,' I said, although feeling I had missed something.

'Then you must see this.' Arnaud suddenly swerved from the main road into wet fields and further on through spindly woods until we came to a pockmarked hill, a car park in front and a granite statue of Marianne, the national symbol of the French Republic. Higher above towered eight stone men. They leaned against each other, one naked with his head thrown back, blank eyes staring out over nothing but lumpy, dark fields, almost the way people stand after an explosion – as I have stood, surprised I am still standing, neither thankful nor with hope.

'They have turned to stone,' Arnaud cried pointing. '*Les Fantômes*. Is this enough? Does this confirm? Do you want to turn into stone? Will you refuse to see anything else? Carole is making a chocolate and pear charlotte for our return. It is warm and dry inside the cottage. Be content. We will go back.'

No, I could not be content. I refused the invitation, and after Arnaud dropped me at Sylvie's cottage, I drove my rental car to the Oise-Aisne American Cemetery, fully intending to find the superintendent and ask to see Section E. The clouds were building again, iron-bottomed with dark, bulbous heads.

The superintendent's residence is a low white building that includes an information centre. It stands opposite the graves on the higher side of the road, and higher still is a grand marble monument on the ridge where the allied forces repelled the German advance.

It was deathly quiet inside the information centre when I arrived, no one in the reception area, just pictorial displays and a coffee table with a huge book resting on top. I leafed through the book, no idea what was in it, my eyes straying to the locked office door and a rear window, glimpses of a backyard. Eventually, a car pulled up and a middle-aged man with very square shoulders and shiny shoes opened the front door. He gave way to an elderly gentleman behind, walking with a cane. They spoke quietly. I tried to listen for American accents, something stupid in my head imagining they'd recognise me as being part of the military because I knew an American who'd been an air force major in the Cold War. At that moment, a young woman rushed in and unlocked the office. I can't give you a good description, only that I recall a high forehead and the air of someone who knew what she was doing. The man with square shoulders addressed her in stumbling French, but she cut him off, saying she spoke English. He asked after a dead relative and in turn she explained an index system cross-referencing names against particular sections, row numbers and graves.

I watched her face, trying to work out if she was friendly. She must have felt me staring and turned.

'Can I help you?'

Her stark expression rattled me, and rather than ask about Section E – not then, not with the two men asking about dead relatives – I blurted that I wanted to find the location of Kilmer's grave.

'Why? Why do you want to know that?' Even the men turned at the force of her response.

I stuttered something about liking poetry – yes, I came from a family who liked poetry. You know that's true – your aunt Alice and your grandfather who scribbled poems at the kitchen table.

'And Kilmer,' I stumbled on, 'I've been wanting to find something. Yesterday, I went to find the Writers Walk in Fismes but—'

'I don't know anything about a Writers Walk, but you're the second person who has asked about Kilmer in as many days,' said the young woman, with narrowing eyes. 'A man came yesterday. If you want to know all about Kilmer, you should talk to him. He brought a piece of cured oak from New Jersey, from where Kilmer was born.' With that she was pulling me in to the office, opening a drawer, showing me the piece of wood and the letter that went with it. 'Yes, this is the man you should talk to. He knows everything about Kilmer. If you want to get in touch, I have his contact details.'

She turned to her desk and held out a business card, the same business card Hermie had given me – the one with the picture of a woman peering through a letterbox, the one I had burned with his postcards.

'Section B, row nine, grave fifteen,' said the young woman.

'What?'

'Kilmer's grave. Do you want to write down his email address? He'll be in France for a little while yet.'

'Who?'

She offered Hermie's business card again.

I pretended to take a photo of it with my phone and then said I didn't need to know about Kilmer in great depth, just thought I'd stop by the grave. What was the location again? She repeated the information and then I think she began telling me something about where they were going to put the piece of oak, and by the time she had said this I realised I'd forgotten the section and row number a second time. I moved towards the door, turned back. 'The location, Section B, row what?'

'Row nine, grave fifteen. The bottom right section. Straight across the road. Dear, oh dear, do you want me to write it on your hand?'

Yes, I would have liked her to write it on my hand because nothing would stay fixed in my head, so I kept reciting the information over and over as I crossed the road to the rows and rows of chunky white crosses with slightly bevelled edges. They reminded me of children's safety furniture, all eerily the same. Then I saw it, a bright handful of flowers in a jam jar in front of Kilmer's cross. Hermie would have left them, so affecting among the monotonous lines, so disturbing too. I ran forward, not sure quite what I was going to do, but in the end snatched them – yes, I stole them. I stole the flowers out of the jam jar and ran to the car. Back in the cottage I arranged them in the coffee press and drank the bottle of champagne Sylvie had left on the counter as a welcoming gift. I also wrote an email to Hermie to tell him I knew he was here, that I'd been to the Oise-Aisne American Cemetery and that I'd snatched his flowers.

So there you go, my darling. I not only tell lies when I panic but am quite capable of being a petty thief. I stole in primary school. The home economics teacher expected students to purchase material to make a blouse. My mother said I would only make a mess of sewing and ordered me to clean up my room. People might think she was cruel, but I knew, even at twelve I knew, there was no money. During the following weeks, when the teacher shouted at me over and over for forgetting, and threatened to ring my mother, I stole coins left on shop counters and desks and in coat pockets until I had enough to buy a square of cheap polyester with tiny yellow flowers. Later, I might have worn the blouse, although my mother didn't ask where it had come from. Both of us looking after each other that way. Sometimes you don't ask.

Sometimes you don't look. Sometimes the reasons for doing anything remain unspoken. As for stealing Hermie's flowers, it felt necessary, almost as if I was saving them, almost as if I was saving myself.

It is nightfall as I write of these things. Beyond the window, the tower of the Romanesque church glows theatrically against the black French sky. It makes me think of the evening you were invited to an event at the Art Gallery of New South Wales. The theme that night was the Moulin Rouge – Baz Luhrmann's film was all the rage that year. Rooms in the art gallery were decked out to look like Parisian streets, small booths selling absinthe cocktails, guests arriving in costume. You chose to wear a long floating tutu, gauze wings on your back – not little girl wings; these rose like a folded butterfly, like fish fins, like a harp. You lay across your wheelchair as if it were a chariot, and I ran behind you over Pyrmont Bridge, past lit fountains, under dark fig trees, along the road bordering the wide lawns of the Domain. Everyone turned, unsure of what they'd seen. The sky was as black as the French sky outside Sylvie's window and you said it looked like a velvet curtain, the stars torn holes.

Glowing sandstone statues in front of the art gallery welcomed you in. Your own exhibition had been a success, tiny etchings printed on giclee paper that resembled the stained-glass windows of a church. Your arms were too weak to paint on a large canvas by then. 'Disability only throws a spotlight on other choices,' you said – those points of light like the stars above the dark fig trees, the footpath sticky with fallen fruit. Bats flew over our heads like winged monkeys and I believed this disease had progressed as far as it could. You had it licked. Your face shone white as a winter moon: too white. I should have noticed it was becoming too white.

In the gloom of Sylvie's kitchen I am seeing another room. It is windowless with green walls. A yellow oyster lamp in the ceiling throws a sickly glow. I see this, although I was never there. I also see the back of Lillian's head, her hair in a French roll. Did she wear her hair that way at that time, or does it simply fit the scene? Your father is beside her, half-turned. You are between them, reclined on your wheelchair like a sphinx. The gastroenterologist behind the desk is saying radioactive imaging has found cancer lesions in your bowel. How can you have cancer? Surely one disease is enough. He says he could remove the lesions but is worried the surgery might kill you, because you can't lie on your curved back to recover and the general anaesthetic might overwhelm your lungs. 'You have two options,' he says. 'You can risk dying on the operating table or endure a long, painful death as the cancer takes its course.'

I don't think you told me for two days.

'Why didn't you tell me you were going for this consultation?' I asked. I hadn't known any of this was happening, any more than I had been brought into the discussion about abandoning a rod in your back.

'Don't go there,' you replied, with 'there' meaning the tension with Lillian.

I should have remained silent, but this time, this time I had to speak. 'How would you feel if it was Lulu?' I asked. 'How would you feel if you didn't know everything there was to know?'

I bent over and began rubbing your back. You were quiet for a while, then said, 'It was like being a contestant on a quiz show. The only choice missing was the mystery box – the one with the surprise inside.'

Later, I heard you were so angry you spun the wheelchair around, hit a chair and smashed open the door. People had to chase you down the corridor.

Did we make up this story? Is it a fairytale about the giants and talking stones told by an excited child who raises the stakes until the giant gets bigger and bigger and the stones turn into a mountain, into a volcano. The breathless child adds on and on. 'And then this happens and then this happens and gorgons appear out of the ground with snake heads.' The hero's chest expands, a shield and cape appear.

You began preparing for the operation: iron infusions to beef up your blood and another type of breathing machine to increase your lung capacity by pushing your ribs in and out. I stood with limp hands. I felt I was in the way of the nurse.

Lillian began the asparagus diet and an expensive regime of acupuncture and Chinese herbs. She was exploring other options as well. Yours was going to be a *Lorenzo's Oil* story. She would be gathering berries in the Himalaya next. Yet I couldn't look for a single berry in that landscape. All I could see was the landscape. Weather rolling in over meadows and streams, and you, one daffodil in a thicket filled with them – daffodils that would go limp in early summer and return again. Why was I wandering through meadows and ravines when others had their laptops open, surfing for solutions?

I rang your uncle and aunt in Canada. Your uncle is a biology expert, and Alice – well, she's a poet, but at least a well-published one, and writes essays about science. I shouted they had to come to Australia now. Everybody had to come.

'Immediately?' Alice replied. She was in the middle of organising a literary festival and needed to find someone to take over. Your uncle – who knows what commitments he had, but it didn't matter because I wasn't listening. This pending operation had eclipsed everything like the white flash of a hydrogen bomb.

They arrived – so did my first son, now found. My brother's daughter cut short a tour in Indonesia and turned up too. Jeff organised a contra deal for rooms in the Ibis Hotel, so we could all be close to the hospital. In return he provided workshops on continuing service improvement to the staff. People waved and smiled at him in the lobby. He's always been so good at tasks.

In the tiny hotel room I grilled my brother for information on every new technology available for cancer. Light therapy was being used in some situations; further experiments were taking place in the United States. I wanted you to be a subject in those experiments. I wanted to use my brother's credentials – a letter to the chief researcher from a senior principal and vice president in an environmental and science engineering firm; that would do the trick. Science, cool and rational;

I would depend on that to still my beating heart. Your grandmother believed in science. She'd worked in a munitions factory near the Clyde River during World War II, prayed German bombs wouldn't take her house overnight. But after the chaos was over, faith in God to hold and preserve was replaced with faith in evidence-based research. Vaccinations stood guard against polio and whooping cough. Antibiotics stopped septicaemia in its tracks. Later, in South Africa, a surgeon would transplant a whole heart. I wanted to believe again that science had all the answers, and opened my laptop to draft a letter for my brother to sign. My sister hovered at my shoulder: 'You've misspelled facioscapulohumeral muscular dystrophy.'

'I've been living with this for years!' I snapped, after she'd come all that way. 'Don't you think I know how to spell it?'

But it was not my fear of the cancer or this operation that made me shout; it was the feeling of being ineffectual. That I got everything wrong. Couldn't even spell. That question I'd asked Louis about finding a way out of the desert. He replied that he'd want his dad to read the map, and while he was figuring out a route, he'd want me to keep him entertained.

Costumes and props, my darling, while, as in Baz Luhrmann's film, real people lie wounded and dying behind the curtain.

I think it was the anaesthetist who buckled and called the operation off. Actually, I can't recall who buckled, although I remember the Chinese acupuncturist, whose rooms were in a shopping mall, saying it was ridiculous acupuncture couldn't be used instead of a general anaesthetic, given anaesthetic was the complicating factor. Your breathing might shut down. Acupuncture was used for major operations in China.

Your father passed this information to the surgical team and I do remember having waves of painful hope and dimly lit horror, and no advice to give either way. As for the research into light therapy in America, the scientist replied to my brother that it was being used for skin cancer but not for the bowel. Even so, it would require cutting you open.

By then, word of the cancer had reached your friends. People turned up at the door with various ideas on cures, including theories about a conspiracy among medical professionals. They only wanted to make money out of surgery and sell drugs. What would they know? One beachcomber – I recall the dangling threads on his cut-off shorts, the bare feet – brought fresh crabs. He spoke of their health properties, told you the best time to catch them was when the tide was coming in. The tide was coming in. The tide was coming in. I felt it. Yellow froth on the waves. Another friend staggered in with a large dispenser of filtered water, plopped it on the kitchen counter beside a vial of colloidal silver. This reminded me of a chemistry set my sister received for Christmas when she was eleven years old – or was it a microscope that came with test tubes containing things to see up close: a dead fly suspended in thick liquid and in another sparkling mineral flakes. The colloidal silver sparkled. Your friend was so confident. Was she the one who sometimes came to do your hair and nails? She unscrewed the cap and mixed the colloidal silver into the filtered water as if she was making a martini, as if she was offering out a new shade of nail varnish, as if she was saying, *darling, it's just your colour and absolutely the rage this year.*

Colloidal silver opens up cancer cells to allow microbes to kill them – at least, that was what I was frantically reading on a website that contained little in the way of statistically meaningful research. I have written on medical matters through the years and can interpret research reports. This seemed like hearsay but there was something about body weight and how much to use, and how it could be contraindicated with particular foods. Had your weight been checked? Had your friend noted the caution about dairy? Earlier, you'd been eating cottage cheese with flaxseed oil, not to mention the American drink filled with shark cartilage. Was shark cartilage contraindicated with colloidal silver? Was it contraindicated with dairy? I slammed my laptop shut.

'Stop!'

I think your friend said, 'Settle, petal, your glasses are fogging up.' But she put down the concoction and left.

Lillian's next approach was to starve the cancer. She banned sugar. She banned red meat. Sugar and red meat cause inflammation and encourage cancer to grow. That was why you still bled despite the regime; it was bits of the tumour breaking away. She also said I needed to be tested for bowel cancer; it was linked to facioscapulohumeral muscular dystrophy. I checked this thoroughly, found other kinds of dystrophies linked to cancer but not ours. I wanted to tell her that she didn't get everything right, but I kept my mouth shut, because I don't know everything either, and at least her conviction was a solid path – and because you wanted to believe in it so much, but would waver. You looked at her. You looked at me. Did I hide my expression? My beloved daughter, it was not simply the cancer, as if there was only a single battle to be won. That's why I offered to take you to Paris. A wild idea, just like you telling me to go to China when the young man from Community Options offered those nine days. Nine days could be forever. Nine days could be a whole life.

Marne Region,
north-eastern France
3 October 2017

It is your birthday. You love cupcakes. You fantasised about visiting the Magnolia Bakery in New York; those girls in *Sex and the City* – you'd be one of them at the counter. Jeff often brought you a box of cupcakes from the Princess Pantry in the mountains: strawberry, lemon, caramel. Your father brought a very chic cake from Zumbo's in Darling Harbour to the transfusion clinic on your birthday, shared it with the nurses. Bought them a coffee maker too. And on another occasion – was it when you had pneumonia? – I remember how he whispered in your ear that you were the kind of girl who believed you could do anything, even walk on the moon, but that today you would need to rest a little. The moon would be tomorrow. Tomorrow you would walk on the moon.

Fairy lights twinkle around your bed. I have turned them on, placed your mobile next to your pillow, and the electric blanket and ceiling fan controls too. The ceiling fan is a gift from Linda and Susan, two women you met in the dog park who invited you back to their airy flat with its magnificent view across the harbour. Susan is a corporate consultant and Linda was once a head nurse, the sort of woman you'd want on a camping expedition. She runs a renovation business now.

Everyone loves you. You have become a darling among the celebrity set after the gallery show, after your drawings appeared on fund-raising Christmas cards. There have been invitations to balls and golf days: you and Lulu on the green, how funny was that? Yet the real performance lay in helping people forget they were speaking to a young woman with twig-thin arms who couldn't sit up and had difficulty speaking because her lips couldn't move. You bore those things for us all somehow. What did you write in one of your poems?

You ask me if I am happy

and every time I wonder

why do you ask

yes

I am happy

everything is fine.

'I can't believe such a large person lives inside such a small body,' one woman in taffeta said after she'd come to visit your flat and left cured of her own angst. But you've always been a changeling. I see you, ten years old at the Sydney Domain, where a speaker stands on orange crates shouting about changes to the national flag. Out on the green lawn a girl in a wheelchair shouts back, 'We're in Australia, not bloody England!' He ignores you at first but finds himself drawn into your argument because of your lucidity, and because others have turned to listen to you. And because in that moment you made the wheelchair disappear.

I worry about leaving you alone in your flat to rest.

'But I like being alone,' you reply. 'There are always so many people coming and going, dishes clattering, the kettle going on and off.'

I clip on Lulu's lead, check that I have the house key, my own mobile and the swipe card that allows me to get in and out of the building, pass the spot in the corridor where Jeff parks his bicycle, wishing he were here. But he doesn't like doing shifts together. He says he has a systems approach and that I interfere with his routine.

The lift shunts down one floor to the lobby. Glass doors open to the street. In one direction the road leads to the Sydney Fish Market, and in the other, towards a dog park circling the harbour. This is a moneyed area now. People with money live here. You live here because developers were required to offer low-cost housing to long-term residents, and you had been on the list for years. It was Jeff who researched suburbs in close proximity to the city when you were desperate to move out on your own – suburbs with wheelchair-accessible footpaths, light rail, and plans for community housing somewhere down the track. Jeff is good with long-term planning. He won the business strategy prize as part of his MBA degree.

The first flat with the pink carpets is not far from here. Back then I was terrified we might not be able to meet the rent if government assistance did not kick in, but it did, and you became eligible for accommodation within the City West Housing scheme. Unlike your first flat and George's creative solution to reversible plumbing, this one is wheelchair accessible and yours forever and ever, as long as forever might be. You are also allowed Lulu; we don't need to hide her anymore. But I think your father believes if you'd never moved out of his house, you would never have caught pneumonia and ended up in hospital for months and months, unable to sit up again. And now that you've been diagnosed with cancer and I have offered to take you to Paris – he says this time I'm going to kill you for sure.

I wish I knew something for sure. I think of myself like one of those fools who climb into a barrel and pitch themselves over Niagara Falls, spinning over the spray. But I think it is in my DNA. Lots of poor people don't plan. What with? They rely on luck. That's why they play the pokies. That's why they throw themselves into the air like a pack of cards. There's the conjurer's magic in my DNA too. My father's mother, an Irish mill girl, which meant half days at school and the rest working in a factory, could turn nothing into something. She'd cover boxes in scraps of sheet, put weeds in an empty milk bottle, make the place look good enough to receive guests, as if there was more in the cupboards behind. And my father himself, a ragtag boy in pants made out of sugar sacking who'd subsisted in the Depression years on bread and jam and anything else he could find in a bin, he could turn dreary into magic too – into an adventure. Those red long johns transforming a dripping ceiling into Santa falling through the roof, the small piece of carpet beneath becoming a boat. We leaped on board, scuffled it forward with our heels. We were off to the hot countries, African explorers. We were fairies flying to the moon. *Let's pretend. Let's pretend. Let's pretend* I can take you to Paris. Let's pretend so hard I can make it real with a happy ending. I don't know if that's possible but I'm committed now. I must hold up the sky, tie the moon and stars in place with thin thread.

What if it breaks?

Louis is enchanted. He wants to come with us to help with heavy lifting. He was thinking of joining the army, had said he wanted a job where he didn't need to make decisions, simply follow orders. I worry about him signing up for Paris, but better Paris than Iraq. Two of your carers volunteer to come too. I've forgotten their names, but the older one I think of as Clemence, her soft heart, her moderation, the way she peeled a piece of fruit with quiet grace. She's cautiously up for this adventure, has never been to Europe. The other one is younger and already helping to plan your wardrobe, her own wardrobe as well. We will need to cover the travel costs of both carers and missed employment opportunities as they will only be caring for you. As for the money to pay for all of this – Jeff is good at high finance. There is talk of mortgaging the house and sponsorship. *Critically ill young woman wants to be in the city of those masters who inspired her art.* He loves extreme events – cycling in the Rocky Mountains, swimming from headland to headland in the Pacific Ocean with the shadow of sharks beneath. But the actual details of this trip, the logistics, and perhaps most of all the emotional weight, are mine. He won't be coming, more like the executive producer who breezes in and out while I tiptoe on a highwire with a brick balanced in either hand. I have flashes of the imminent fall: landing in Paris, rain streaming from a black sky, air traffic controllers waving torches, someone calling an ambulance and you rushed to hospital where no one in emergency has seen your condition before. Yet doggedly I take the next step, because you are having so much fun imagining another landing where we will stroll the cobblestone streets of Montmartre, drink *café au lait* and crumble chocolate croissants.

But, but, but … you also hesitate in that dizzying space between the imagined and real, so we have breathing tests to see if you can handle the air pressure on the flight. We contact the muscular dystrophy specialist, tell him what we are doing and that we will need your medical history and contacts in France. I expect him to say we were crazy. But he doesn't.

In this scene we are going to his office to pick up those files. Your father will meet us as well. Did you ask him? It is just you and me in the wheelchair taxi with an Iranian driver who was forced to flee his beloved country. He was a professor of philosophy there. You've booked him many times, and on this trip he is comparing Arabic and English, how in Arabic the moon is masculine and the sun feminine, how there is a word that describes the wave in a woman's hair, not a curl but a wave, so the meaning can also signify a broken promise in love. He drives slowly and carefully as he tells us these things, knowing each bump in the road can hurt your back.

Your attention is elsewhere. Should you go to Paris? Should you stay? You wish God or the universe would give us a sign. I stare at the rear-view mirror. Youths in the car behind are following too closely, arms draped out the windows, music thumping, and edging to pass. Suddenly they are beside us, the driver shaking his fist. When we come to a red traffic light, he jumps out, throws his face against our driver's window and screams, 'I'll fuckin' rip youse head off.' The light turns green and we begin moving again, still slowly and carefully, still mindful of you in the back, while the youths drive on with rude fingers in the air.

'You are going to Paris,' says your specialist, his face lit with a bright smile. Your drawings hang on his wall. The medical notes compiled for our journey lie on his desk. He has also contacted a colleague in France.

Your father appears in the corridor, apologises for being late. Why am I relieved to see him? He takes a chair next to me just as we sat next to each other to hear your diagnosis all those years ago.

You are quiet, staring down at the lowered backrest of the wheelchair in the same way Lulu stares at her empty plate. Or does Lulu resemble you? She rolls her eyes in the same way.

'I'm on a special diet,' you say, looking up now at the specialist. 'Do you think natural therapies can cure cancer?'

He replies that you look very well. Indeed, he's never seen you looking so good. This is true. You skin blooms. Lillian's diet.

Your father finally speaks. 'Can travel compromise her health?'

The specialist is such a mild-mannered man. 'There is always a risk with travel,' he replies, without suggesting a decision either way. 'It puts the body under stress.'

Clemence was on shift when we returned. She helped you out of your wheelchair and into bed. I was due to go home. She came out of your room as I was filling my backpack, a wrinkle in her mind. She'd spoken to her daughter.

'Did you know that there are trip advisors for people with disabilities? They charge a fee, but…'

I looked up. Oh, how I wanted this. An expert. Someone to vet decisions and help me plan. Clemence had a number. I rang right away and she appeared the next day, bustling in, all pink cheeks and strawberry hair and settling herself at the dining table with a checklist. Travel insurance was at the top of her list. I assured her it was the first thing I'd locked in when exploring flights.

'They approved you?' Her eyebrows shot up. 'Which insurance company?'

I didn't have the name on hand but said I would ring the travel agent later to check.

'Could you ring her now?'

'Right this minute?'

She nodded.

I rang the travel agent, the one who was checking with airlines about removing seats to fit in your wheelchair.

'I'll check with the insurance company again,' she said. 'Will ring right back.'

'She's checking,' I said to the travel advisor, who'd turned back to her list. 'Let's run down the rest of the boxes, shall we? Tick them off.'

Her list was nowhere near as comprehensive as the list in my head. Your requirements were like no one else's: the wheelchair with a lowered backrest that didn't fit standard wheelchair taxis, beds at a very specific height that allowed you to balance on your toes when sliding onto a commode, a carer inside the shower stall with you, so a shower stall big enough for two. We would need to puree food, so a food processor in the room.

As I explained these things, the travel agent rang back. 'I misunderstood,' she said, like a school kid who'd used the wrong colour pen. 'The insurers can't provide the cover.'

Without missing a beat, the trip advisor suggested a holiday in Britain. 'Australia has a reciprocal health care agreement with them,' she said cheerfully. But I knew you weren't interested in Britain; we'd discussed this before. It had to be Paris. *La Ville Lumière*.

'Well, I suppose if she does get sick you could catch a fast train to London,' said the advisor, stacking her forms.

'But if you go by ambulance, or if you got stuck in a French hospital it will bankrupt you. Then again there are other insurance companies. I'll email some names. Give that a whirl.'

At this point you called from the bedroom. You were covered in blankets, your voice muffled under the mask.

'What's going on?'

I led the trip advisor to the door and returned, bent over your bed. 'There's a problem with the travel insurance,' I said, 'but I'm not giving up. There are other avenues.'

You pulled the mask away. 'No,' you said, the word breathy with all that air pumping around. 'It's the sign. We'll go when I'm better.'

And so we came down from the sky and entered the trenches. Was Lillian's strategy going to be a success? You kept asking me to prod your stomach. Had the tumour grown? Had it shrunk? Lillian said it had shrunk.

What could I reply? Sometimes I felt a lump. Was it food? I'm not a doctor and was confused as to what signalled progress. Did you tell me the gastroenterologist said it had shrunk and that was good, or that someone else had said the cancer diet caused the tumour to grow larger before it collapsed?

Nurses came to take blood samples. I checked the mailbox for the results. 'Are the results back?' you asked almost the moment you woke. The cancer markers went up and down, just as the tumour seemed to grow and shrink, although one nurse told me that taking a blood sample was like drawing water from a river. Sometimes it captures more debris; sometimes it captures less.

When the cancer markers went down, you relaxed a tiny bit – had a taste of something you shouldn't, or didn't finish the American shark powder drink, which was vile and thick.

'Do I have to drink it all?'

You wanted me to say you didn't need to do everything Lillian had prescribed, and yet if I did, it would mean I didn't believe in her cancer cure regime, and you would hate me for that.

You woke at night shouting into your mask with bad dreams, night-time shadows stretching over the flat's concrete walls, painted the colour of nothing, the matching carpet that held every stain. This may be your flat for ever and ever, but subsidised housing comes with woeful décor and rules that nothing can be changed. I decided if we had to wait until you'd beaten cancer before going to Paris, then I must bring Paris to you.

Linda snapped up the idea, said she could get free paint through her renovations business – then the offer extended to free light fixtures and tradies to do the job. Next, we were talking about plantation shutters for your bedroom, ripping up the carpet and putting down a floating wood floor. A wood floor would be easier to clean.

I was sick to the stomach at the thought of asking permission from City West Housing to redecorate. How many times had I gone down to their office to apologise about carers losing security swipe cards, parking in the wrong spot, or the late submission of doctors' certificates confirming you were still disabled so your rent contribution remained the same? Now I was going to ask if we could rip out the carpet, put in a floating floor, change the lighting fixtures, paint your walls turquoise and lilac.

The City West office had a sliding glass window and a buzzer to let them know you are there.

'Yes?'

Did one of them come out into the lobby as I began to explain? Was this too much to discuss through a glass slot? I only remember at the end I was speaking through clenched teeth. 'I will sign a legal document guaranteeing we will turn everything back to exactly the way it was before. EVERYTHING! It needs to be Paris up there. It needs to be all of bloody France!'

Dearest daughter, I am in France, the bloodiest part. Even after a century there are still craters where the bombs fell, slender grass and daisies trying to soften the effect. Hermie has replied. No mention of the stolen flowers. He wrote to say he's been out seeing people, making contacts, hardly remembered I was in France because he's been so busy with his own research. But hey, now that my email popped up, he still has to visit the St. Mihiel American Cemetery and will be passing my village. He might drop by if there's time. Tomorrow or the day after, take my pick.

I wrote back that the day after would suit best, not wanting to seem too keen – hating him, and wanting him to come. Not wanting him to come. He feels like a boulder, stony and smug. I want to bite him but would only break my teeth. In Berlin he told me he was frightened of my teeth. It was when I was running my mouth over his ears, his neck, his torso. He suddenly grabbed my head and pulled my face away, and yet when I left the bed, he reached for me and pinned me back down at his side. We clawed at each other as if what I was fighting was inside him and what he was fighting was inside me, and so it continued and continues.

Marne Region,
north-eastern France
4 October 2017

Sylvie came earlier to fix the side gate. It had fallen off its hinges. She was carrying a drill. The red scarf back around her head bobbed up and down as if the rain had left a flabby balloon in its wake.

I was already up when I caught sight of her, had showered, brushed my teeth and wiped the table clear of sticky circles. The clean-up effort was a result of Hermie's reply to my email about going to the Oise-Aisne American Cemetery– oh, why did I write it? I've only made a fool of myself. But perhaps mentioning stealing the flowers could be construed as a light-hearted joke. Do you think it sounded like a joke? In Berlin I told him I used to steal things. Perhaps he will remember and laugh. If he comes tomorrow, I could make a crack about Eddie Slovik saying he'd been executed by the military, not for desertion, but for stealing gum, and then wish him well with his own research. As for me, why I'd come to France despite our falling out – I could say an editor had asked me to write a journal article about interpretations of war. Oh, I know, I know, there was no such request, but I have been exploring the subject to some extent, don't you think? Those thoughts on Menelaus and the Trojan battles? I could also mention the washhouses. This morning I've been researching washhouses, feeling ashamed (is that the word? or do I mean exposed) by the way I behaved with Arnaud in Courville and then running away after he'd taken me to see the stone statues.

The washhouse in Courville was erected in memory of Lieutenant William Muir Russel, a young American pilot who'd crashed near the village in a dog fight in 1918. Courville suffered terribly in World War I under the German scorched earth policy, buildings gratuitously dynamited on their retreat. Two years later, Russel's father travelled to collect his son's body but fell fatally ill in a New York hotel. There he wrote a last will and testament, leaving money to the village and asking them to honour his boy with some sort of improvement, a fountain perhaps. The money funded a system to bring water into the town; the fountain was built with a much-required washhouse at the rear and that incongruous American eagle on top. War is so incongruous, don't you think?

Hermie said if you live long enough to survive a war, you might later see its purpose. I think by that he meant how the aftermath encourages us to reflect on the nature of the beast, which is a strange, constructed thing. We are left wondering what was battled and defeated. You battled the cancer, but you never took up arms against the muscular dystrophy, did you. You ignored suggested exercises following the pneumonia. You let your body take on the shape of the progress of that disease. People said how it was a shame, how beautiful you would have been without the defective gene.

'Muscular dystrophy shaped me,' you answered in reply. 'It's who I am, and I like who I am. I extend the possibilities of what it means to be human.'

Oh, darling, there is so much beauty in that.

As for that beast growing up from your bowels like an Odyssean creature rising from the Underworld, you turned that battle into a festive outing – had us all dolled up in bright red lipstick and 1950s sundresses for iron infusions at the hospital clinic. Just loved the funky little nurse who flung back his black hair and warbled, 'Welcome, ladies,' when we arrived. How brilliant was he at sliding a cannula into the back of your hand, laying out the equipment as if it was cutlery, as if this was fine dining, as if we were in the Sydney Cove Oyster Bar.

But on this day, the one that comes to mind, he was on holiday and a pretty blond thing, frightened of your thin hand, stuffed up the insertion again and again. She became so flustered she rang a veteran from the Emergency Department, one of those gals who's seen everything: snake bites, people who've been struck by lightning, legs torn off and worse. She snapped on latex gloves. 'Which is your good hand?' Your head hovered mournfully over the bruises and blood spots. 'It used to be that one,' you replied.

Gawd, you are droll.

Your ankle was hurting too, twinges that had started earlier in the week every time you put pressure on the supporting foot to slide off the commode to the mattress. Your carers had started lifting you – well, more of a small lurch forward, up and over. I asked the visiting home doctor about your ankle. I can't remember if it was a he or a she; they rotated. Get used to one and a new face appeared. *Can something be done for her ankle?* But there was no protocol for people with a seriously advanced form of facioscapulohumeral muscular dystrophy, who have elected not to have a steel rod in their back and still retain some use of their legs, and now balance off the side of their mattress on one foot because they can't lie on their stomach any longer due to a cancer tumour in their abdomen that can't be excised.

I began ringing physiotherapists to ask for advice – I mean, you see those movies with paraplegics in swimming pools, fit instructors holding them under their chins. Couldn't you do that to give your ankles some relief? But each receptionist told me I would need to bring you in for assessment and you couldn't bear the thought of travelling to lie in a waiting room, only to be told they had no idea how to help.

It was Clemence who said she'd passed a physiotherapy clinic in a lane behind the old convict church across the road. This was news to me, although there are lots of hidden lanes in inner Sydney: alleyways for night-soil men in years gone by. In the 1800s, priests in that church were instructed to report people and activities dangerous to the Christian faith: the Communist Party, gambling, drink and sailors.

Do you remember attending a carol service at that church on Christmas Eve? I know you were hoping for magic in the flickering candles, the way the parishioners helped lift your electric wheelchair over the worn steps.

'There.' Clemence pointed through the kitchen window. She was getting ready to leave. 'The lane is between those terraces. Hard to see it behind the vine.'

Yes, I suddenly saw it as if she'd made it appear.

Once you were settled down for a nap, I hurried towards that opening, half-expecting to be transported back in time to when ragged kids played cricket, kids whose parents had been transported to the colonies for petty theft. But there it was at the rear of a narrow yard. I stumbled through the door, began blurting your story to the receptionist: your muscular dystrophy, the cancer, the ankle, and how I couldn't stay away long because you were back there. I jabbed my finger in the direction of the lane. Pushy, desperate, but if people only knew all the doors knocked on, all those who had cut me off before I could explain – all the times I've gone through your situation only to discover I was standing in the wrong queue and would need to start again. And the god-awful relief when someone listens and accommodates. Isn't it lovely to remember the dentist who moved his furniture around to allow your wheelchair in the room and then got down on his knees to examine your mouth, because these things are not difficult, these things are hardly out of one's way. You drew him a small picture of a tooth fairy convention as a thankyou gift.

'He's with a patient now,' said the receptionist kindly. 'I'll send a text to let him know you are here.'

A door opposite opened. The physiotherapist was on his knees, a small man with a face like a friendly seal. On a chair was an elderly man with bloated legs, his trousers rolled up. 'It's okay, love,' said the elderly patient. 'I can wait.' And they both waited while I explained all over again.

The physiotherapist came to your flat. I watched as he turned your ankles gently and massaged your lower back and legs. 'Hopefully a little relief for now,' he said. 'It could be stress-related from balancing like that so long.' He placed his thumb and forefinger on your neck, close to where your shoulder bones spiked around your ears. 'Don't your shoulders hurt?'

'I've got used it,' you replied. 'It's best not to pay attention.'

He recommended an ankle support, scribbled down different suppliers because we would need to experiment to find one that fit. He also suggested memory foam for under your elbows and feet. He turned to me. 'Cortisone shots could assist if the ankle joint is severely inflamed. We need an X-ray as well, preferably an MRI. Her foot could be fractured. Is there a chance it may be fractured?'

I ordered three different ankle supports and rang Dunlop. They were out of memory foam, but your story so distressed the manager he drove all the way to a supplier to pick up a piece as big as a mattress and deliver it to your door. Your father was there when it arrived. He carved squares to fit under your feet, smaller ones for your elbows. But it didn't help, did it. You needed to lean on hard surfaces to balance. The ankle supports didn't work either. No one has such a thin ankle, such a thin foot.

As for the MRI scan, there was something complicated in getting one, something about the cost, something about this not being inside your care program – but that was the cancer care program. And this strikes me now with such clarity. How your cancer team seemed to have forgotten the muscular dystrophy was progressing too. I rang the muscle specialist we'd consulted when you were planning the trip to France. He was situated in a different hospital within a different health care district. His people would need to speak to their people, and that would mean working across disciplines and funding boundaries. But he would start the process. While all of this was going on, the woman who owned the agency providing your carer support rang to say it had come to her attention you were being lifted off the shower chair and commode. It wasn't allowed.

'It's not really a lift,' I replied. I was standing in my own kitchen. The sun was so terribly bright, glancing off the kettle. 'It's just a little lurch that allows her to flop onto the mattress without putting so much strain on her ankle.'

'It's not allowed. No one will be doing it again.'

'But how will she get on and off the commode?'

'She won't.'

The silence that followed felt like finding potatoes in the cupboard that had gone to seed, crumpled skins and wormy shoots. It felt like the time I saw you as a little girl in the bathtub, the shadow of your scapula starting to wing. It feels like Hermie's tired flower bouquet wilting beside me in a glass, the slimy stems and one bright daisy bravely standing.

It was Louis who saw the expression on my face when he walked in the door. He hadn't joined the army. We hadn't gone to France. Instead he'd applied to work at a facility for the severely disabled.

He didn't say much when I told him; he never says much in the moment but later he broke down at work. He hadn't told his manager about you. She spoke to their occupational therapist; lifting equipment had advanced. He rang me to chat about your situation and new designs, although any equipment would need to be approved by an occupational therapist in your district and legal lifting requirements.

So here we are in the living area of your flat: the district occupational therapist, just out of training, a hoist salesman, the carer agency manager, Louis and me. Clemence and you are in your room. The hoist salesman begins attaching metal rods to a mesh hammock. The occupational therapist turns to Louis. 'Show us how the family perform a lift.' (The family are allowed. It's our backs.)

We all crowd into your bedroom to watch Louis slide you on and off the shower chair, that tiny lurch. Then he demonstrates a complete lift. He uses one arm to support your hips, another to support your rib cage, lifts you off the bed. Your legs and arms fall like a rag doll. He is so gentle with his big sister, the one who made cakes with him, played *Final Fantasy VII* throughout a summer holiday while I was at work.

'This is how our device will hold you as well,' says the salesman. He asks Louis to carry you to the living area and lower you over the hammock. Once you are on the floor he hooks the metal bars to a large frame and cranks a lever. You cry out. Any fool can see you are collapsing in the middle. The hoist is made for someone with a straight backbone, and the mesh and bars are not the same as the tension in your brother's arms.

'Give it a minute,' he says. 'This will work.'

It is like watching a crane in a wrecking yard lift a crushed car. 'Stop!' I shout. 'You're hurting her!'

The moment you touch the floor you begin offering suggestions about the placement of the suspension rods, the length of the net. You are good at engineering solutions, the way you adapted your wheelchair. But the occupational therapist has already packed away her clipboard, and soon she and most of the others have left. It's just you and me, and Clemence. She helps you onto the commode. She shouldn't because even if it is such a tiny lurch she won't be able to claim workers compensation if she injures herself.

'For heaven's sake,' she says, as she guides you over the mattress. 'I'd be putting myself in more danger trying to hook that thing up.'

The hoist remained in the living room over the weeks to come, I can't recall why. Maybe it was because the salesman had to run to another appointment and didn't have enough time to take it apart again, or maybe he half-listened to you and thought you might come up with an idea.

You've had a hoist in your flat before. It was after the bout of pneumonia. That hoist had a pink foam harness. You twirled in circles when the lever was cranked. 'A circus act,' you said, after the experiment. 'We should have made it a ticketed event.'

That hoist stayed in your flat for a lengthy period as well, suggesting a problem had been solved. At Christmas we strung lights around it, hung coloured glass balls. It looked quite lovely, a sculpture, the pink leather. It matched one of the lamps.

Marne Region,
north-eastern France
6 October 2017

Where to begin taking you through the last two days? Yesterday, at first light I pulled on my coat to stomp along a muddy side road that runs through rutted fields and was surprised to see a young woman wearing slip-on sandals and stretchy purple leggings, as if she'd only just left her bed too. Two large dogs were with her, their bushy tails swishing and her bottom jiggling like a happy baby's just out of the bath. Every so often the dogs ran into the middle of the road, which was dangerous if a car happened to come. Cars don't come often but can appear with little warning. The young woman pulled off a sandal, raised it threateningly. The dogs cowered, slunk back, then wagged their tails. Somehow this made me feel happy, the ease of the scold and then all forgiven. I longed to be easygoing like her, like the dogs. An easygoing person would have tea in the house for a guest – biscuits, things like that, serve it casually, say goodbye and get on with her day. I decided that was the best approach with Hermie and returned to take stock of what was in the cupboard and fridge: two carrots, an apple and piece of cheese. The rest of the stale baguette. There was also the powdered soup and the tin of butter beans, hardly the stuff of afternoon tea. I considered buying another apple and perhaps a pastry in the village where the old woman sells vegetables.

I left mid-morning – the *boulangerie* closed at noon. Once there I spent the longest time staring at two chiffon slices in the window, the thought of buying them suddenly a decision of overwhelming proportions. Should I buy two? Two would suggest that I expected Hermie to arrive. I bought one and a baguette, forgot about the apple and drove back to Sylvie's cottage, where I threw the wilting flowers in the rubbish bin – although I did save the single surviving daisy and put it in a small glass. The chiffon slice went in the fridge, where it sat alone on a shelf in a way that made me want to burst into tears. By then it was approaching half past one. Should I go for another walk? Instead I sat at the table watching the hands of the large kitchen clock turning and listening to new guests move in next door. There were bursts of female laughter but I didn't look outside to see who belonged to the noise.

At three-thirty a tap came to my door. It wasn't Hermie; it was Arnaud and Carole with half the chocolate and pear charlotte wrapped in foil. 'Too much for us,' Carole said, and then commented on the door being slightly ajar, which it was in case Hermie arrived.

'You must lock your door,' she said. 'Anyone could turn up. Arnaud told me about the van driver, giving your address out so easily like that.'

My heart pounded. I didn't want Hermie to appear and Carole and Arnaud to think —oh gawd, what might they think? Carole handed me the charlotte. 'You look tired,' she said. 'We don't need to come in.'

I laughed, one of those fake nervous laughs, and replied that I was in the middle of researching washhouses and that I'd love to share my findings. 'Perhaps I could walk around,' I said. 'Maybe tomorrow?' I turned to Arnaud. 'I apologise for the way I behaved after the trip to Courville. I should have rung to explain. A message came into my phone when we were in the cathedral. It was from my sister. I misread it and assumed she was in crisis in Canada, but she wasn't.' I laughed again.

They both took this in politely, knowing it wasn't true, but I kept up the charade, then made an exhibition of locking the door behind them, laughing through the tiny grate and saying I hoped they'd heard the click. After they left, I ate a large slice of the charlotte standing at the counter, then went downstairs and arranged the magazines and tourist brochures. By then it was ten to four, but four arrived and no other knock came. Then it was five and then six. I opened the fridge to look at the chiffon slice sitting alone on the shelf and told myself I didn't care, until at six-thirty there was another rap on the now locked door. I rushed down the steps. This time it was three young women who stood there. The one in front had fair hair and a light blouse, pale yellow I think. The ones behind wore dark dresses like widows or resigned spinsters, young and old at the same time. They began speaking rapidly in French while the one in front, who spoke English, blushed deeply. 'My cousins had no idea anyone was living next door. They thought the man who came to our *gîte* was looking for me, and kept telling him I would be back soon. Poor man he kept returning again and again.' She held out a note. 'He gave them this.'

It was Hermie's handwriting. That tiny script I recognised from his Berlin postcards. *Hey, a man came to your door selling Bibles, but you were out. Tried lots of times.*

I darted out, swung my head to the left and right, taking in the grassy square in front of the cottage and the road leading out, desperate to see a parked car. 'Is he still here? Is he coming back?'

'No,' she replied. 'He finally left. He came and went for over two hours.'

I thanked her and ran to my laptop. I'd shut down Google Hangouts during the same fit when I burned his postcards. I scrambled to set it up again then typed: *I don't know if this program works. You knocked on the wrong door. Please come back.*

I'm not sure what I did after that. I may have walked up and down the stairs sixteen times. Then I opened my laptop again and began writing the most desperate email about how I didn't believe in love either but must see him one last time to say goodbye. Too many things had disappeared out of my life when I wasn't looking. I had to touch his face again.

As I began typing I heard a ping. The green light in the Google Hangouts bar appeared. He was online. Then those bouncing balls as he typed a message.

Shit, I only read this now.

I typed underneath. *I will drive to visit you tonight. Or would you come here? I have food.*

Shit again. Then how maybe he could grab some things, sleep over and go to the St. Mihiel American Cemetery the next day. He hadn't made it today. If I had food, he had some wine. *Goddammit*, he wrote. *I'm tired.*

You could eat and then sleep, I replied.

A slight pause and then the bouncing balls.

We'll see about sleeping. And then the green light went off.

It was dark when I heard the tap, just the stars and the lights on the Romanesque church. Hermie was holding a box of pastries. I grabbed his coat and pulled him in from the night, pushed him against the wall and began kissing his cheeks, his ears, and nipping his lips in fury. The pastry box wobbled.

'Wait.' He lowered it to the floor. Then he was kissing me, tossing me back and forth so that he could reach every side of my face and my neck, his hands sliding under my clothes. But it was more of a wrestle than lovemaking.

'Just for France,' he muttered between breaths.

'Just for France,' I muttered back.

I felt the weight of him, the soft lips, the hard teeth beneath. He smelled of soap. He is very clean.

This morning I woke behind his pale back, left him sleeping and came down to the kitchen, to the table with the blue and white patterned tablecloth, my notebooks and the box of pastries.

Hermie appeared as I was writing, fastened his belt buckle and announced it was too late now to go to Saint-Mihiel, as if this was all my fault. Then, as he was stuffing items into his backpack, he said, 'There is an archaeological museum in Soissons with an exhibition of artefacts recovered from World War I. I'll go there instead and afterwards visit the tenant farmer and his wife at Muercy Farm near where Kilmer was shot. They've been so helpful. That's why I bought the pastries. I bought the cakes for them, and tomorrow I'll head to Saint- Mihiel. There was a battle close to that American cemetery too.'

'Yes,' I replied. 'You already said.'

I wondered if he knew about Section E or had seen it, but I wasn't going to ask him, not with his face like that. 'I suppose you receive a great welcome at the cemeteries,' I continued, waiting for the smirk. Instead, something like humiliation crossed his face.

'Some of those cemetery superintendents are ex-marines,' he replied. 'They only tolerate me.'

This left me feeling confused. 'Why?'

He began a diatribe then about who had earned their stripes, and how he hadn't earned the right kind, then something about military honour and the *Bhagavad Gita*, a sacred Indian text about a prince who was filled with doubt on the battlefield, and then circled round to his obsession with Father Duffy again, how he'd gone in with his soldiers without a rifle and carried the wounded back to safety. I couldn't follow where he was going with all of this, but I could feel the heat in it, the questioning, the wanting to do the right thing, to know one's proper role.

He is gone now, and I have come down to the sitting room to sit and stare. The sky is low. It promises to rain again, although every so often watery sunlight breaks through. I am filled with longing for something I can't name and that Hermie hasn't provided or won't.

Traces de la Guerre still lies on the table beside the tourist brochures I stacked neatly the other day. I have looked at some of them. I could drive to the Ruinart Champagne House and wander through its underground chalk tunnels or head to Fort de la Pompelle that houses a collection of over five hundred Imperial German Army helmets, lots of artillery too, although the brochure that caught my attention most was l'abbaye Notre Dame du Val d'Igny Something about the abbey's quiet endurance. It was first built in the twelfth century, suffered through the One Hundred Years War and the French Wars of Religion and the Franco-Spanish War – looted, destroyed and rebuilt over and over. In 1914, the Germans took over and turned it into a hospital for infectious disease, and then, retreating from the Battle of the Marne, blew it up. Once again it was restored and now houses a community of Cistercian nuns who carry on a long tradition of making chocolates. There are pictures at the back of the brochure of the chocolates. Some are shaped like champagne corks and filled with liqueur. I imagine buying you one. You would nibble it slowly, wouldn't you. I never knew a woman who demonstrated such restraint with chocolate. I'd wolf a box down in one go. But of course sweets weren't allowed on Lillian's diet.

Was it winter when we decided to postpone the trip to France to allow her regime to work? I think it was winter in Sydney – not cold like Canada but still cool enough for the cafés on Harris Street to drag oil-burning heat lamps onto footpaths. I see them at twilight, glowing like torches, or small campfires. You would ask me to run to the shops while you slept – more asparagus, more sticky patches to protect your face from the pressure of the CPAP mask. The mask was winning over the mouth plate by then, that silk scarf draped over your dressing table mirror; you didn't want to see your face anymore.

You came to stay with me in the mountains when renovations began, and Linda supervised painters, electricians and flooring people to tear apart your flat. City West contacted me regularly to complain about tradies taking parking spots. Linda rang to complain that City West were being rude to the tradies, and how terrible this was because they'd donated their services for free.

I assembled a bed for you in my kitchen, holding the fantasy you could spend time there during the day. We would chat while I blended asparagus. You thought this was how it might be as well, just as on a previous Christmas when you came to the mountains, you thought we would sit outside at the Bon Ton restaurant and eat ice cream under the great oak tree. But if you recall, by that Christmas you weren't really well enough to do those things. We did take the wheelchair to the shaded park at the end of the street. I brought the camera and took photos of Lulu and you in the dappled light. I was hoping to catch you at gentle angles so that later we would remember the day as being something other than it really was, which was you staring at the ground, your hand on the knob that controlled the wheelchair, tired beyond tired and trying to wring something lovely out of the day. You liked the little yellow flowers, you told me later. You liked looking at them.

After you went home to the redecorated flat, to the silver wallpaper sourced by a friend in London, to the plantation shutters, to the lilac walls and new brass bed, we hosted that cocktail party, and a few months later your father rang. I was curled up in the corner chair near my kitchen. I'd hung crystals on threads from the curtain rails, the walls shot with twirling rainbows.

Your father is prone to yelling when he is stressed, but this time his voice was deathly calm. 'She's been taken into hospital again,' he said. 'You need to come.'

I did not rush that time. I did not screech down the highway. I did not swerve in and out of the passing lane as I have done on the other occasions, when a carer rang. The sky was achingly blue, and I was taking in the yellow flowers in the grassy swale that lined the road, yellow flowers that resemble the ones growing here in France but withering now as colder weather arrives. Seasons are turning, the way seasons must turn, and I recall the Jehovah's Witnesses who came to my door when you were a teenager, saw you in the wheelchair. 'God has his reasons,' they said.

'God? God wanted this?' I spoke with menace. 'If God ordained this, then I hate him, but what you witness is not what I see. I see a field of flowers and the mass of them is so beautiful and she is one. She is one of the flowers. They don't come in the same shape, and seasons turn, and the flowers come up again.'

Am I in France remembering these things?

I am everywhere and anywhere arriving in an emergency room where a mother holds a child with a fevered face and partners clutch each other's hands. But I can't see Jeff, even though I'd rung him before I left for the hospital, even though he was in the city and could have been here long before me.

A nurse buzzes me into a corridor, your father stands at a second door, holding it open, waving me in. His eyes are slits in a puffed face. He takes me to your bed behind a curtain. Two of your carers are there, and Lillian, and your younger sister, and the half-brother with the shy eyes. You are wearing your CPAP breathing mask and have been crying. I come behind and begin rubbing your lower back. Now Jeff appears in his lycra bicycle gear holding a takeaway coffee. Louis and Max appear too, because I rang them. They shuffle into the circle around your bed. How many? Ten. There are ten people around your bed.

Your gastroenterologist, an older man with eyes like a faithful dog, kneels in front of you. A young woman with skin as translucent as bone porcelain is at my back. She is a surgeon. She says she will go ahead and perform a colostomy without general anaesthetic because you are going to die now if nothing is done. But you have to understand the local anaesthetic can still interfere with your breathing and given you don't want to be hooked up to a breathing machine for the rest of your life, without intubation you might die then and there. You will need to remain calm during the operation. She can't risk you hyperventilating.

Your gastroenterologist beseeches you not to have the surgery, to choose palliative care. But I watch as your love of life turns you into a Spartan, adrenaline pumping in the narrow pass at Thermopylae. Yes, a scene in a movie, and movies end well. We are just in the battle sequence now. Victory will prevail.

Lillian bustles to prepare you, hands your rings to your sister for safekeeping and then turns to me. She never turns to me.

'Only one family member is allowed in the operating room with her,' she says. 'It must be you. You brought her into the world. You must be with her if she goes out.'

Jeff is on the phone, calling the world, telling people what is happening. But he doesn't see what is really happening, this thing Lillian has said, which takes my breath away. An honoured commission to a less-than soldier who does not believe this battle will go well. Did you want me to be the one? You turn to the surgeon and ask if Jeff could come in as well because he lifts you best. The surgeon hands him a blue paper hat. Jeff seems pleased with the uniform and Lillian, I see her so clearly now, her inner tension held in elegant calm, working on sign language: one finger when the discomfort increases to the slightly unbearable, two if the surgeons need to give you a chance to catch your breath. Three if you can't take it anymore.

Too soon, an orderly wheels you into a corridor, because everything must happen now. But I don't see you entering that operating room in Sydney. I see a door opening into Canada, into Southern Ontario where you were born, where people go camping and paddle around the myriad of rivers and lakes in canoes. You and I are camping. A blue tent has been arranged over the top part of your body and I am in the tent as well, girl scouts on holiday. We are being tested on the semaphore system, although in this case you are using fingers instead of flags. Raise one. Raise two.

Your hair is damp. I wonder if this is because you have been swimming or is it due to the thunderstorm pelting the sides of the tent, just as there was a thunderstorm that hot night at the end of summer when you were born, your face and hair just as damp and slick. You could have died in my birth canal. But you survived that dark night and this one too.

It was quiet in intensive care after everyone else had left, just the nurses' soft shuffle and the beeps from machines. I stayed. I wanted to stay, your slim fingers locked through mine, your eyes opening and closing in this aftermath. Why am I reminded of a horse brought down on a battlefield? That creature so large and you so small but your eyes with the same mute stare. If there were guns, they were far away by then.

I think your father may have come to relieve me in the morning, and may have come late, but I was not rushing to leave. It was only when Jeff arrived – he'd been sleeping at your flat and would take me there while he went to a meeting, or some such thing – that I realised I was exhausted, too exhausted to sleep. I lay in the carers' bed until he returned and by then was desperately hungry. The sequence of what followed is muddled in memory, only that we ended up in a cafeteria below the offices where he worked. He was part of a human resources team consulting on organisational change within a health facility – and your story, the fact that he had a stepdaughter whose disability had been complicated with cancer – I think added to his authenticity. He was close to a true front line and facing real management issues every day.

Where was the front line? I was still scanning for the front line. I saw daylight, big glass cafeteria windows and the barista making flat whites, short blacks, cappuccinos. Sandwiches lay on glass shelves: shaved ham and mustard on panini; pesto and turkey with camembert. Office workers formed a queue and perhaps there were outpatients and families there as well. It didn't feel like the front line; it felt like the world ticking over in peacetime.

Jeff moved out of the queue to speak to an employee he knew. Was he telling last night's story? I had a sense it had already been announced and this was the morning recap – the breakfast program hosts chatting about highlights from last night's football match with a bleary-eyed forward who has a shot at the John Eales Medal. Advertisements for kitchen appliances or bodybuilding equipment would follow.

Jeff's fine hands, his clean nails, the line of his pressed shirt cuff against his wrist. Did I tell you his hands were one of the things I fell in love with? The way he rests them on the steering wheel, the way he shuffles cards. He loves bridge and often wins, gets angry when he loses after playing all the correct cards and others haven't dealt the logical hand. What are the correct cards?

I can't rouse myself to chat with this employee. I don't want to speak of last night, that battle; the experience is too rare, and Jeff cannot see me anyway. I've vanished. I am not here in this cafeteria; I am back on the battlefield with you, your flanks shuddering, your nostrils flared. Still alive for now.

It is close to midnight. I have returned to this letter. Hermie is sleeping upstairs after coming in earlier and finding me in a terrible mood, drunk with my head on the table. He sent a message about three hours after he left this morning: *Hi. My friend at Muercy Farm dug up an artillery shell while ploughing the field. There are bullet holes in the barn as well. I'm heading to Soissons now and afterwards might come over and 'ahem' shack up with you before heading to Saint-Mihiel tomorrow.*

Jesus wept. We may not be doing romance, but I'm not an order-out pizza. I didn't reply. Instead, I decided to go somewhere too. Damned if I was going to be here if he came knocking at the door. I settled on the abbey. It was close enough and the general layout of this region is starting to shrink to a manageable shape in my brain, the squares of yellow fields, the wooded hollows dappled like the setting for a teddy bears' picnic, and a little ominous as well: Red Riding Hood, Hansel and Gretel, and that tale about the red shoes. Do you remember that story about the little girl who was so in love with her dancing shoes that she wore them to church?

'What pretty shoes,' the minister said, or perhaps a priest – I can't recall, only that the shoes snapped fast to her feet, began tapping on their own, forcing the little girl to dance too. On and on they clattered away from the church and out and over the yellow fields until she met a woodcutter, and begged him to chop off her feet. Still the shoes raced away, the bloodied stumps inside, dancing, dancing, dancing. The story holds such a grim fascination. Is it something to do with a body going on without heart, without mind, without soul?

I was thinking about this, thinking about you when I approached the abbey. It stood like a fortress among the trees, a stone tower with twelve gothic windows, and rows of outer buildings with pitched roofs. An elderly monk strolled along a path. Like that time when I first discovered how ill you were, I had an overwhelming desire to run towards him, fall on my knees and beg permission to stay forever. Let me make chocolates and chant. He was tall, very tall but with the demeanour of a boy who doesn't quite know how to be in a long body. Giant sandals on his giant feet. He turned, such a sweet, open face, to tell me in such an apologetic tone that I'd missed a tour but there were historical display boards inside. There was also a gift shop. He pointed in its direction.

'Do nuns work in the shop?' I asked.

'*Bien sur*,' he replied, a little startled, and added in English. 'In the chocolate factory too. But it is closed today.'

There was one nun behind the counter and another stocking shelves. I pretended to browse a display of silver-plated chains, each holding a pendant containing a bluish stone. Held to the light the stone reflected a hologram of a woman's face. This was supposed to be the Madonna's spirit encased in rock. I brought one to the counter along with a box of chocolates and a bottle of lemon liqueur. I was thinking the necklace would make you laugh. Do you remember that well-meaning friend who gave you a religious calendar with a statue of the Virgin Mary superimposed against vacation spots? The Virgin Mary floating over the Grand Canyon, the Virgin Mary floating over the Tower of Pisa, the Virgin Mary floating over the Taj Mahal. We rolled about in hysterics. Still, we did not throw it out, or the holy water she brought in a plastic drink bottle. We tied a ribbon around the cap and kept it close.

The nun smiled at my purchase and began adding up price tags.

I asked, 'Can divorced women join the order?'

She glanced up, startled like the monk. 'They can follow our path, but—'

'Can you have your own room?' I interrupted. 'Work in the chocolate factory?'

She answered slowly in English, a gentle frown furrowing. 'We have people who are not nuns who help.' She began putting my purchases in a paper bag.

'The necklace is for my daughter,' I said, as if this explained my questions.

She paused, tucked a postcard of the Virgin Mary into the bag. 'I hope she likes the necklace,' she said, handing the package forward. 'I hope it blesses her. I hope wearing it gives her grace and peace.'

I am not filled with grace and peace. When I got back to Sylvie's cottage I drank three glasses of the liqueur. Hermie had sent another message: *Been driving the fuck all over the place in the rain, got lost and never made Soissons. Instead bought some food to make you dinner. May I come soon to knock on your door?*

I didn't reply, instead drank more liqueur and brought up the page on my laptop where I'd been reading soldiers' letters from the Front. This one from Private Terry:

We have just come out of the trenches after being in for six days and up to our waists in water. While we were in the trenches one of the Germans came over to our trench for a cigarette and then back again, and he was not fired at. We and the Germans started walking about in the open between the two trenches, repairing them, and there was no firing at all. I think they are all getting fed up with it.

You had a second colostomy without general anaesthetic. The first one became blocked. Your father and Lillian went in with you that time, holes in both sides of your torso like pursed pink mouths. We crossed paths in the hospital, bumped into each other in the lift: yellow chrysanthemums and happy balloons. One particular morning I arrived to find a policeman in the hospital corridor with a gun. A wounded prisoner was in the room adjoining yours. Something behind the wall clanged like broken plumbing. Clang. Clang. Clang.

'They've handcuffed him to the bed,' you said, when you saw the question on my face. 'All night long it's been going on. He's trying to shake himself free.'

The plumbing in my mountain cottage had begun to crack, those two events coming together in my memory now. I don't think I said anything to you about the plumbing at the time but surely you will remember the state of the bathroom and laundry area at the back of the house – how decades ago a previous owner slapped a tin roof over what had been an outdoor dunny, fitted a washing machine and toilet into one area, and a shower and bath opposite. The nailed-in windows wouldn't open. Black mildew speckled the ceilings. The walls had separated from the floor. Spiders and cockroaches crawled in.

Do you remember the day I worked my way around the skirting boards of your flat with a can of insect spray cursing the Buddhist twins' shrines, the little slices of apple? They were attracting cockroaches and I worried they'd crawl inside your CPAP machine. They were shocked, said they'd smelled death all the way down the corridor.

'Okay,' I barked back. Flipped through the *Yellow Pages* and found a pest control company that laid down organic traps.

'If the cockroaches eat the stuff it's their choice,' I said, showing them the ad. 'They're probably hoping to be reborn as some higher form of life.'

You laughed and laughed in the other room.

As for the bathroom and laundry in the mountain cottage, you recommended building a decorative barrier out of steel wool and bricks. You were good at homemade building solutions. When the chip-wood cupboards in my kitchen bubbled up with damp, you suggested I patch the holes with papier-mâché, cover it all with a coat of shellac. That was the time when you were big on shellac and gesso, having used them in your paintings, and I was big on cement. I propped up the sagging benchtop over those cupboards with the broken end of a broom and smoothed cement into a wavy pattern to hide the gap between the counter and wall. 'Very Gaudi,' you said. 'Very Casa Batlló.' We hung one of your paintings above.

But some things lay beyond our reach: the plumbing, the holes in your sides –although people were saying brightly that colostomies could be reversed.

Over those weeks the dripping in the bathroom became worse. It became harder and harder to turn off the leaking taps. I was using pliers by then, put a bucket under the showerhead, used the water to splash on plants. Eventually, Jeff asked me to ring the plumber; he'd had enough of it himself. But I wonder at my waiting for him to see it as a problem, as if I couldn't be fed up on my own. Was it his ability to read maps, add up figures quickly, that left me believing he had the most reasoned response to everything else?

The plumber arrived, a cranky man, the kind who makes you feel as if broken tap seals are your fault, sort of like the dentist who asks harshly if you've been flossing your teeth.

He took off the showerhead, waved a torch into the cavity behind. 'Nothing holding those pipes,' he said, telling me to look in as well. 'The whole wall is ready to collapse. The pipes are ready to go too.'

Jeff suggested putting a shower in the laundry and letting the bathroom area collapse. I see him holding a measuring tape while I stare at the ceiling trying to imagine the roof suspended over that section as the walls fall away. In the kitchen, forms for the National Disability Insurance Scheme lie on the table; the legislation has come through. Jeff was in like a shot to ensure you became test case number one. I was supposed to fill in questions about your career goals and the support people you would need to achieve them. You could shuffle the money around any way you liked, hire a secretary if that's what you wanted, get rid of your existing carers and look at cheaper options. Jeff said new immigrants came cheap. He said I could train them up.

I'd been ignoring those forms, just as Jeff had been ignoring the crumbling back of the house. But at this moment I see now he is pushing them in front of me, insistent, frustrated that I haven't completed them yet. But I can't see through the words on the paper, can't see you hiring a secretary to achieve your career goals, can't see you replacing Clemence or the other carers who have become your friends.

And now I see something else, although it is not inside the mountain cottage. It is in an X-ray room. Your wheelchair is positioned next to the technician's cubicle. He has asked me to take off your shoes. They are your pink ballet slippers that never wear out. The muscle specialist organised this X-ray to see what could be done about your ankle. Phosphorus images appear on the screen. When I was a little girl in Scotland, shoe shops had X-ray machines to check children's feet were sitting properly in their brand new shoes. Of course, no one would use an X-ray machine so carelessly now. I hold your foot in position, ask the technician what he sees.

Facioscapulohumeral muscular dystrophy is linked with osteoporosis. There are hairline fractures in your ankles and feet. Everything is cracking.

The builder places plastic sheeting over the great gaping hole between the laundry area and the corridor. He needs to bulldoze the cement floor. He is on a list for a knee replacement and limps back and forth. I am in the corridor trying to make a neat pattern around the plastic with masking tape.

I am trying to make the hole look nice.

The jackhammering continues. Rat-ta-ta-tat-tat. Then stops. The builder reappears on my side of the plastic with his labourer, a wiry young man wearing plug earrings, a cigarette between his lips. 'White ants. We have to stop.' He is holding grubs in a jar, says he needs to call the council inspector, says the whole back of the house has to come down.

There are more forms on the dining room table now. A loan application to cover this extended construction. Proof of our income. Our tax returns. Those documents lie beside the application for your place in the National Disability Insurance Scheme. Jeff is there, and I say, 'I hope the bank will approve the loan because at this point we don't have working plumbing in the bathroom or a laundry.'

Suddenly Jeff is saying he doesn't want to live in the cottage, or with me.

It was easy for Hermie to walk in this evening. I hadn't locked the door. He'd brought fresh salmon, carrots and leeks, which he began quietly slicing on the kitchen counter as if he had not stormed off earlier in the day or found it odd to see me sleeping off the effects of sweet liqueur. I didn't raise my head, but sensing I was awake, he asked if I might like to go with him to Soissons in the morning, see the Archaeological Museum. We could take his car. It had a built-in GPS.

I growled into my elbow that no one drives me anywhere anymore. If I went, it would be in my car with him in the passenger seat and me behind the wheel.

'With the grill smashed in like that?'

'Yes, with the grill smashed in like that.'

He shrugged and when the meal he was cooking was ready he carried it downstairs to the sitting room, which he called the dungeon. He'd downloaded a movie on his laptop, a Peanuts movie, *It's the Great Pumpkin, Charlie Brown*.

'Well, it is Halloween at the end of the month,' he said, arranging plates on the coffee table and pouring himself a measure of the liqueur. The cartoon came on in bright block colours, carrying me back to when I was a new kid in Canada scampering through a cold night with devils and angels and ballerinas. We raced into the custard warmth of apartment blocks, up and down stairs. All year long we'd plan our costumes, *I will be. I will be.* We were immigrant kids in crepe paper living in purpose-built flats. We were scurrying across cement parking lots, past trash cans and an overturned shopping trolley at the lip of a dark ravine.

Did you ever watch the *Great Pumpkin*? I don't think the movie was as popular in Australia or made as much sense. Most Australians think Halloween is an American invention but I remember celebrating it in Scotland, although not with a glut of sweets. The adults were all part of the fun, bobbing for apples and treacle scones on a string. You had to sing or do a wee dance to get a treat. Halloween was about marking the line between one year's harvest and the cold winter that would follow prior to spring, a time when the veil between living and death is thinnest. Hermie turned to me during the film. 'Charles Schulz, the creator of Peanuts, was wrestling with faith when he wrote the *Great Pumpkin*,' he said. 'I watch this every year.'

In the movie, Linus sits in a pumpkin patch waiting for the Great Pumpkin, whom he believes will bring a sack of toys for all good girls and boys who have faith that he will appear, even if he's never appeared yet. Meanwhile, the other kids are getting ready to go door to door in their costumes for guaranteed treats. They think he's nuts. Snoopy is dressed as a World War I flying ace, imagining himself tiptoeing through the battlefields of France.

In the final scene, Linus is deserted by Sally, his one follower. He wails after her into the dark night, 'And if the Great Pumpkin comes—' He claps his hand over his mouth. 'If?' he whispers, hoping no one has heard. 'Did I say if?'

Dearest, I have been tiptoeing through the battlefields of France in a crepe paper costume that bleeds in the rain. I have come home to a jagged mouth in a pumpkin shell and my mother sitting on the sofa, her legs folded under her like a girl, her hands smelling of dishwater, her apron still on. She has stopped to watch the Peanuts movie too. She loves movies. She believes in them. She devours them like boiled sweets. My little brother is dressed as a World War I flying ace, put my father's industrial goggles on his head. All three of us are following a cartoon dog through the battlefields of France.

Let's pretend. Let's be. Late one night a cartoon character popped out of your pen: dots for eyes, no mouth, crazy hair. You sent her off on adventures with her little dog. They tried their hand at being mermaids (too fishy), fairies (too many wishes to grant). They travelled to London and China in hot air balloons – lived in teapots, sat in a Parisian café, tied stars on string and hung them in the night sky on Christmas Eve.

Marne Region,
north-eastern France
7 October 2017

Hermie bought a lapel pin today in Soissons. I've been turning it over in my hand. The pin is a miniature replica of a spiked German Pickelhaube helmet, a M15 Adrian helmet and the British Brodie helmet welded together in a row. Hermie said the Brodie helmet is known as the Doughboy helmet in America. He was thrilled to find a souvenir commemorating all three major combatants on the Western Front. 'In the following world war my maternal and paternal grandfathers fought on opposite sides,' he said at the cash register. 'Only found out when they met at my parents' wedding. There was a stunned silence, a laugh and then a beer.'

Hermie has returned to his own lodgings. He said he didn't want to worry the owner with his absence. 'It's nowhere near as fancy as your place,' he added. 'But I like it better.' Gosh, he pisses me off, the way he overshares opinions. When we were in Soissons he barked information like I was in bootcamp, or worse – like he was up in the pulpit lecturing the congregation below. And you know how that goes with me. The format of sermons as if this is the one and only way to interpret a biblical story. No room for questions or comments from the floor.

We went to Soissons first thing this morning. Lots of stone buttresses, winged statues and the Aisne River reflecting a row of Lombardy poplar trees. Gold leaves flamed upwards as if they were on fire. The Abbey of Saint-Léger is riddled with bullet holes. The Archaeological Museum sits behind. It's built out of pig metal to resemble an old bunker. Only the top floor pokes out of the ground.

We found the display of war relics in the windowless basement. A photograph of skeletons in a ditch covers a complete wall. This was the remains of the Lincolnshire Regiment linked elbow to elbow and found near Arras. Hermie began taking notes but I was feeling claustrophobic and began moving quickly from chamber to chamber. It was like being in a dark cave. Glass cases held recovered bits of uniform, helmets and barbed wire, or metal bramble as it was known as then. Some twenty-four thousand tonnes of it were removed from the Nord-Pas-de-Calais region alone. There were more photos of soldiers eating together, digging ditches together, carrying mates on stretchers – and past those, a video clip of a flamethrower, a weapon that directs a stream of blazing oil. Another glass case held ink pots and pens. Ink pots and writing implements were found all over the Marne, perhaps as common as bones. A photograph showed a soldier sitting at a makeshift desk. He had a pipe in his mouth, knitted socks. It could have been my father at the kitchen table, that look of contemplation. He'd been a soldier too; fought in World War II, wild with grief that his older brother had been killed in Egypt. His brother would have done just about anything to be free of the Clydebank, tried to sign up with the Big Brother movement when he was sixteen. It would have taken him to Australia. But your great-grandmother wouldn't sign the papers, and the following year, when he enlisted in the army, she marched down to the recruiting station. 'He's too young,' she shouted. Still, they kept him, told her he'd be trained and sent into battle when he was of age. A grenade blew him to bits at El Alamein.

He had been your great-grandmother's favourite son. The one learning to be an electrician who'd rewired her tiny council cottage. As for my father – oh, he was good at papering walls and charming her with poetry. But he wasn't smart enough to rewire a house.

My father was smart enough to know the accuracy rating of the guns on board the merchant ships he manned had an error margin so wide they couldn't have hit the blind side of a bus. The sailors were simply waving them at the tracer flames. Oh, the idiocy of it all. Suddenly I had to sit down on the floor. My stomach turned. My mouth was so dry.

How do I write from our front, my darling? You, like a soldier up to your waist in water or hiding in bombed-out houses, dodging the flamethrowers. What was that like?

Your father, Lillian and I were becoming numb. I can't speak for Jeff; he has this uncanny ability to keep doing things, as if these things are normal, as if it is normal to be up to one's waist in water for six days. As if you can make a poached egg on toast and read the morning paper from that position. But somehow he did.

One night you began choking while slurping the shark powder drink. The carer couldn't find the suction machine and rang me. 'Three minutes,' I screamed, not remembering where it was. 'We have three minutes. Press the VitalCall button!'

I held on to the phone, rocking on my haunches, until I heard crashing that indicated the paramedics were there. It was me who had put the suction machine in your wardrobe when I was vacuuming. You who said you didn't want it on the counter when guests arrived. I had forgotten. The horrid selfish words I'd whispered to Jeff. 'I will be blamed. They will say this is my fault.'

I said the same when your grandmother had cancer and I was spooning water through her parched lips. Some spilled into her mouth too quickly and she began to choke. I ran into the corridor screaming for a nurse.

'Help. Help. I'm killing my mother!'

A nurse appeared, a large woman with firm hands. She took hold of my shoulders and shook me gently. 'Sh-sh.

Cancer is killing your mother, my dear, and there's not a darn thing you can do about it.'

Yes, sh-sh-sh indeed. Yet Lillian had researched a radio wave machine that would zap cancer cells without the need for surgery or drugs. It was going to cost thousands of dollars. Jeff was in training for the Big Red Ride, everyone chasing a cure for cancer. As for me, I had spent money on chandeliers, pasted decals on your window of the Eiffel Tower and a little bird singing in a cage. I'd walked door to door over two afternoons gathering signatures to support the National Disability Insurance Scheme. The scheme would allow people with disabilities to manage their own funding, purchase services and resources in whatever mix suited them best. Isn't that what any of us want? A little control over our resources? But I didn't want to have these kinds of philosophical conversations on doorsteps. Nor did I want to hold up your story as an example of the benefits of allowing young people to live independently rather than be shunted away to nursing homes, because somehow it felt like it would be holding me up as well: heroic mother. I was no hero and had been told I'd lost the right to call myself your mother time and time again. Still you were my heart, and if I'd run around carrying political flags or raising money for charity, it would have taken away precious time being with you. An afternoon spent placing decals on your window. The melting sunlight that day. Lulu's pink nose.

Hermie found me crouched on the floor of the museum. 'The air,' I said. 'It's stuffy here.'

'It's because you refused breakfast,' he said, pulling me to my feet and marching me across to a bar-restaurant, only to discover most of the menu applied to dinner. It was barely noon. He ordered croque monsieur from the snack menu, which is more or less a ham and cheese sandwich smothered in bechamel sauce. I had the croque madame, which is basically the same thing with an egg replacing the ham.

Hermie left to use the washrooms just as the dishes arrived, and in his absence I took a photo of the food. I do my best to take photos of meals for you. I've taken one of scrambled eggs that I microwaved in a cup. That photo was taken in Paris, where I stayed for two nights, exhausted after flying from Australia. Mind you, it didn't feel as if I'd landed in Paris; I've been more firmly located in that city inside your flat. Most of the time I lay on the bed inside the small room, only venturing out to buy the eggs, and once to a café across the road where I ate chipped beef and raisins wrapped in pastry. I took a photo of the chipped beef and raisins too. The waiter saw me and smirked. Stupid tourist.

When I took the photo of the croque madame, a man at the next table glanced up, an older man with shaggy hair who appeared to be composing music on a laptop. Not wanting him to think I was a stupid tourist I said something about researching metaphors of war, although what cheese sandwiches had to do with war was anyone's guess. He didn't seem perturbed by my odd explanation and in turn replied that he was a professor of music and found it ironic the British were listening to Wagner just as World War I was taking shape.

When Hermie appeared, the conversation turned to his play and the ink pots and other writing implements he'd seen in the museum. This rankled because it felt he and he alone had seen them, and wanting to feel relevant I mentioned Arnaud and the Writers Walk. I hadn't mentioned Arnaud up to that point. I'm not sure why, perhaps because I hadn't found the installation. And what did that say? I thought of Sylvie's dismissive comment. She knew the location of cemeteries and battles. Carole knew the names of troops and bombed buildings. I'd gone looking for the Writers Walk and ended up in a bog finding nothing, yet on the way I'd seen – even now those slender trees come to mind, the sunlight slanting through.

Hermie swivelled in his chair. 'A Writers Walk. Hell, I need to see that.'

I regretted saying anything. 'It isn't there,' I snapped, angry because I felt he would find it, but not in the way I'd find it, if that makes any sense. I'm tired of other people telling me what to see and how to see it. What's significant and what is not.

'What do you mean it isn't there?'

'I've looked.'

'Have you asked this Arnaud guy again? Maybe you were looking in the wrong place.'

'What does that mean?' I spat back.

There was a moment of awkward silence. The professor said he needed to pack up.

Hermie and I returned to the car. I didn't turn on the ignition, felt my breath coming in and out as if I was squeezing air through a thin straw.

'Do you want to swap seats?' Hermie asked after a few moments. 'I can drive. Look, I don't know what set you off. I'll look the display up, track it down myself.'

'Fuck that,' I replied and turned on the ignition.

There was roadwork between Soissons and Fismes too. I was glad the GPS was broken. It would have been no use at all, some disembodied voice droning *Re-routing, Re-routing, Make a U-turn,* or a sudden alert that you were not on a road at all, when there was a goddamn road; you're driving on it. I knew where to go, ground into second gear, booted the car up a slope.

'What?' Hermie shouted. 'What are you so pissed about?'

'Global positioning systems. Those stupid voices that think they know the right direction.'

He snorted. 'You can never know anything. You only come to believe things. You do that by poking your finger into the world.'

He had the good sense not to speak the rest of the way. I parked in the square close to a monument not far from where I'd previously crashed the car. There are always monuments in France, this one shaped like a thin pyramid and an inscription that read, *La Ville de Fismes et ses Enfants*, followed by a list of those lost to war. For me the word 'enfants' always conjures up images of your brothers as children, Max's freckled ankles, the earnest part in Louis's hair. Christopher made me a tiny clay bowl for my earrings when he was six, gave it to me a week after Mother's Day when his visit was due. 'It wobbles,' he said, placing the bowl and a handmade card on my bedside table. 'But you could put a rock on one side to make it stand straight.'

Boys always seem more vulnerable, don't you think? The way they carry a teacup to a sick relative, their hands too clumsy for bone china. Tea slopping into the saucer, puddled and brown. Yet in the end this is always what it comes to in war: the mopping of brows of the wounded and sick, and waiting, waiting for a call to action when this is the only action to be done.

I didn't want to stand shivering in the wind while Hermie took photos of a bleak monument from every angle, instead turned towards a street I thought would take me directly to the river, one that would avoid the twists and turns from the day I ended in a bog. Hermie followed eventually, barking at me to get onto the footpath because I was walking on the road. But I wanted to see clearly round corners. I didn't want anyone telling me I was going the wrong way. He didn't. By then he was taking in the flat-faced stone houses and stopped at a brass plaque fixed to a pillar beside a driveway. *Passant, souviens-toi*. A command using the sweetly personal form of the word 'you'. *You who are passing by remember this*. The mayor of Fismes, Doctor Genillon, had lived in the house. He was arrested for acts of resistance against the German occupation during World War II, and deported to a Nazi concentration camp.

Fismes was totally destroyed in World War I, and then because it was an important transportation site, it was rebuilt in the years between. Oh, how we define our enemies over and over again. In World War II the Vichy government aligned itself with the Nazis. I could almost hear the clickity-clack of train wheels passing through the station, the cattle cars, the people crushed inside.

Almost a year ago, when I dragged my suitcase from the Schönhauser Allee Station in Berlin to the one-room flat in a side street, I saw similar brass plaques on the entry steps. Two young women with flaxen hair were polishing them on their knees. Later, when I left to meet Hermie on the railway overpass I saw burning candles beside them in metal cups. Hermie told me the plaques were engraved with the names of Jews snatched from the building, people who had lived in the very room where I slept. He brought pastries that day too and then sat at the table as I fell asleep on the bed. I didn't hear him leave, only saw the message on the corner of an envelope, his tiny script again. *I am so happy just to sit in this chair and listen to you breathe.*

In Fismes I continued to walk a little in front of him, not looking behind to see if he was still there. We came to the bridge. I mounted the steel steps and walked towards the café where the young waiter had been so kind. The monuments erected by the State of Pennsylvania loomed large at the other end. I left Hermie to stare at the monument and rounded the bridge to slide to the riverbank below. Hermie crouched to pick at something in a way that reminded me of how he'd dug bottle tops out of the asphalt in Berlin. He held it up. 'A bullet casing?' It turned out to be a seashell. Since his arrival, he has spoken so often of wanting to hold evidence in his hand, to touch this war, to know it this way. More importantly, he wanted to find it himself as if someone from the Front had stretched out a hand and offered it through the centuries, making them as one. He called out again.

'That's the Vesle River where you are standing. Can you imagine? So peaceful now but soldiers were crawling through those nettles back then.' He pointed towards the thick mat close to my feet. The river shimmered. Memory shimmered too. I was back in a hospital room but not with you. It was the day I thought I'd hastened your grandmother's death by spilling too much water into her mouth. She did die later that afternoon. My sister and brother were there. We sang her favourite songs because it was something we could offer in circumstances beyond our control. She breathed in a rasping way, shuddered, lay still and became chalk white, like a seashell, like a fairy thing one might find inside a flower, or beside a creek at the bottom of the ravine where my sister and I had collected leaves, odd-shaped stones, flowers – and once the slim bone from a dead bird's wing. As I stood next to your grandmother, I found myself back in that ravine – this bone-white form I'd found, bird wing that was also stone, flower and leaf. Out of my throat came the words, *of course*, because at that moment I felt myself inside her body, felt myself all of these things too. The life I was living was no more than a dream, a story I'd made up, as fleeting as a spider skating on a pond.

I remember waking one spring morning at sixteen and registering the incredible luck of finding myself in a young body with all my life ahead. Now I wake in Sylvie's cottage in autumn, the world in a terrible autumn; we have used up so much. If it had been your dream, my dearest, would you have made a better fist of things? Oh, how I wish I could have given my body to you.

I looked down again at the Vesle River, the green mat. Nettles? They weren't nettles. The leaves looked so richly green and soft. I crouched to grab a handful, felt nothing at first and then an explosion of burning pain. At that moment I also saw a display board in the shadow of the bridge, *Les Pas des Écrivains en Guerre*, Footsteps of Writers at War.

'I can't believe you did that!' Hermie shouted from the top of the bridge. 'I can't believe you grabbed them when I told you what they were!'

My hand was burning. I wanted it to burn. I wanted to feel the pain of this, my burning hand while I stood watching the Vesle River shimmering silver ribbons.

Hermie was keen to walk the route. But I had taken in enough for one day. I told him I would go with him tomorrow. Now I am alone in the dungeon room. Funny how the room takes on a different ambience with his renaming. Funny how anything can be framed and reframed. An amber lamp in the corner is casting a particular glow I can't quite describe. The pear tree beyond the French doors has become a scarecrow shadow, the stone shed a pale gloom. Hermie's lapel pin could be anything – a paper clip, or the hard back of a beetle.

I have been reading about war again.

There are at least six articles open in my browser. This

one an interview with Marjorie Miller about the challenges of covering the Iraq war. Miller was a foreign correspondent for the *LA Times* for seventeen years. She speaks about getting as many viewpoints on events as possible. In the case of the Iraq war some journalists remained in Baghdad throughout the conflict. Some were embedded with the US military and some came in behind. Others went into Kurdish areas on their own. There were journalists in surrounding countries too.

Miller says the problem with reporting from one position is that you only get a little piece of the story. The news received doesn't necessarily conflict, but a journalist can only report on what he or she sees. Miller's job was to feed the news elements into a larger story, where she could balance the relative importance and points of view.

What is the larger story of us? Have you got a grasp on that from where you are now? What am I supposed to see? Something about the stinging nettles, then seeing the sign for the Writers Walk – as if you are shouting down from the sky. 'See this. Feel that. It's not one thing or the other. Listen to Arnaud. It's the all-ness of things.'

What is the contributing news, the individual elements from where I was stationed?

Jeff packed a bag and left. We met a few weeks later in central Sydney at Relationships Australia. My idea. The marriage counselling service was having a promotional deal. First session no charge. Afterwards, Jeff asked if I wanted to go for a cup of tea. I followed him through the streets, our bodies reflected on the ground floor windows of office towers, zigzagged and stretched. In Starbucks he ordered at the counter while I sat in a booth. When he brought the mugs to the table, he said while he was in the shower that morning, he realised he was going to die.

'It was a visceral feeling,' he whispered with astonishment, and I was astonished in turn that he was well into his fifth decade and the thought hadn't gripped him before. He also told me that I needed to understand he'd never loved me. 'I only came to Australia for an adventure.'

I've been turning that exchange over and over. *I only came for an adventure*. Who was Jeff? He's there in the letters that I've been writing to you, but he isn't there, is he. Not fully fleshed out. More like Dudley Do-Right of the Mounties, making an appearance and gone. I can't ever remember him looking into my eyes and asking in any intimate kind of way, *and how are you?*

Many were outraged that Jeff would leave at such a time and I did bring up the topic with Hermie in a veiled way – not mentioning Jeff specifically, but during one of Hermie's rants about good soldiers, I asked what he thought of soldiers who desert.

'It's not all about God and Country out on the battlefield,' he replied. 'It's about loyalty to your fellow soldiers. You don't desert them.'

I've been musing about the noble vision of God and Country, where afterwards you stand on a platform and get medals pinned to your chest. It's much more performative in a very public sense than the complex cohesion of a troop, where valour is often hidden from the wider view. Was Jeff ever part of a troop? As much as I warred with your father, it strikes me now how we were connected, Lillian and me too – because we were so deeply mired in the overwhelming feelings of war. Not better people in what we did but terribly authentic in our exchange.

I only came for an adventure. Lots of young men who signed up for battle have said the same thing. As for Jeff saying he realised he was going to die, I thought of what I've been reading about those who are gung-ho in military training often being the first to desert the battlefield when it got real. And it did get so real, my dearest. That operation when Jeff placed you on the table. You and I got to stay in the tent practising semaphore signals. It was Jeff who watched the surgeons slice open your stomach, lift out your bowel.

In an interview veteran journalist Charles Glass has spoken about desertion. In the case of Private Weiss, the soldier simply wandered off in the middle of the night in a daze. Others recounted a similar experience. They hadn't made a conscious decision to desert, only found their bodies leading them away from the Front.

In the end the same thing happened to me, my darling, but then I think I did something worse. I think I joined the enemy camp.

Marne Region,
north-eastern France
8 October 2017

I have road rash on my knees. There are still bits of grit in the cuts. I can almost hear my mother hollering, 'Why did you do that to yourself?' She'd be dragging me over to the sink, roughly scrubbing a wet washer into the sores. 'Stand still!'

This afternoon, Hermie shouted at me before he understood what I was babbling about after falling into a deep hole. He is sleeping upstairs again and I want to show you my knees, as if we were girls in a sleepover and earlier I'd come tumbling off my bike. Then you might show me the scar on your arm and the other one on your thigh. How many scars have we got? Let's count them.

Hermie and I returned to Fismes today. We traced the Writers Walk along the river, up through backyard vegetable plots, and over to the other side of town. I put my nose to a garden fence, a serene row of cabbages behind, and next to me a display board with photos of shattered trees, dead horses, and one wall standing like the craggy pinnacle of a drilled tooth.

The display boards were numbered but spread a fair way apart. It wasn't always clear where we should head next. In the town, boards nine to eleven went missing, but Hermie was familiar with the geography of the battle and this is what we seemed to be following – stages of the conflict mapped out.

He pointed to a rise above the town. 'I'm pretty sure that's where the Allied forces had their lookout.' He marched off in that direction while still scanning the ground. He was so hopeful still that he might spot the edge of a rifle, a helmet, a buckle, a belt. We came to an open bald space with a clear view of the village below and a tangle of bushes to the right. Hermie plunged in. I followed. He was sliding into a deep hollow. I remained at the rim.

'A trench?' I called down, wondering how soldiers scrambled up the sides to shoot and then imagined I could see soldiers crouched with rifles – or did the lumps of stone, splintered twigs suggest something else? A wet patch gleamed like an eye.

Hermie was at the bottom by then. 'No,' he called back. 'This could be a bomb crater.' He peered up at the sky. And with that I peered up too, lost my footing, felt an explosion shudder my bones. Everything splintering.

I became stick thin after Jeff left, although not as thin as you. Your father took over his shifts. I see him in your kitchen, pureeing asparagus, his overnight case packed and in the hallway. Lulu is next to his feet. Her tail drops when she sees me come in. She knows this means I'm taking over. There will be no more treats. I have pasted vet's guidelines on the refrigerator, underlined them in red: A TINY SQUARE OF CHEESE IS EQUAL TO FOUR HAMBURGERS IN A SMALL DOG.

This is the war now.

Your father turns back to the asparagus, spoons it into plastic containers that he will forget to date. He moves towards the refrigerator, the one with new glass shelves, and opens a freezer stuffed with ice cream, pizzas and frozen meat pies. He can't help buying this stuff. It's as if he's expecting a famine, and now he's trying to push in the containers of asparagus. But they won't fit. He removes the pizzas and chucks them in the bin.

'Those were a mistake,' he says, closing the lid.

Lulu glances at me as if this is my fault.

'Why, do they taste awful?' I ask, surprised I've said anything at all.

'No,' he replies. 'Because I'm fat enough as it is.'

I look up from where I've crouched to remove my shoes. This man with his overnight case in the hallway, the dog staring at him with beseeching eyes.

'You're just fine,' I say, and mean it.

Was that switching sides – joining the enemy team? Max was beside himself over his father's departure, punched a hole in the kitchen wall. Louis – oh, Louis, whom I'd asked when he was just eleven and you were in intensive care why we'd been sent so many challenges.

'I guess the universe thinks we're the sort of people who can take it,' he said.

We couldn't.

It was close to December. My sister Alice arrived. You'd emailed her secretly. *You need to come.* Alice accompanied me to your flat, held her hands open like a nursing assistant as she watched me lift you. You didn't quite trust her to do it just yet.

Early summer rain fell in torrents. The train to and from the city and mountains was continually held up. Sometimes it took us three hours to get home. The builders were still tearing up the white ant damage. The floor in the corridor had been jackhammered away. Alice and I balanced on exposed beams around the edges to reach the crumbling bathroom. At least the toilet in there still worked. She was shocked when she saw me undress.

'Oh God. You are skin and bones.'

But I couldn't eat, couldn't sleep. Alice tried blending smoothies, but they wouldn't go down. Next, she dragged me to the medical centre, insisted on blood tests.

'Her organs are dissolving,' said the doctor reading the results. 'Keep this up and we'll need to put her on a drip. It happens when a person gets shock after shock. The body goes into survival mode. You don't see an animal eating when it's scanning for wolves.'

We walked out with a script for antidepressants. I took one that night, but my skin was crawling the next day. 'Give it time to work,' Alice said. But I wouldn't. And still it rained and rained and rained.

Late one afternoon, Lillian arrived at your flat with her own sister to take over our shift. I remember them both staring at me intently, not with malice, but with the same expression as a relief brigade not wishing to give away how awful the remaining soldiers look, how ragged. I know I looked ragged by then.

The telephone rang just as Alice and I were gathering our belongings to head for the train. It was the owner of the carer services. She needed to draw up the Christmas roster. What days could I do?

I'm not sure who took the call. Was it me? Was it Lillian? Or did I relay the questions to Lillian holding the phone to my chest? I do recall an exchange about the cost of holiday hours, about how much money was in your care payment plan, about Lillian's family commitments, which she was discussing with her own sister.

For myself I didn't care what was sorted. No amount of sorting would pave any road out of here. There were just tasks to perform. Your flat smelled of face washers. Everything smelled like face washers now, and this parleying back and forth about dates and shifts. What did it matter? I just wanted instructions on what to do. The next thing I heard was Alice's voice. 'This is madness. I'm taking my sister to hospital. Someone else needs to figure this out.'

I panicked, remembering the home for unwed mothers, feeling I was going to be locked away again. But Alice showed me a brochure that reminded me of 1930s movies where people with tuberculosis stay in large white mansions overlooking the sea. I imagined a nurse wearing a white cap spreading a tartan rug over my knees. In the evening there would be a room of my own, a lamp, a fluttering moth.

The woman who greeted us in the waiting area – her face now gone from my mind – took us on a tour through polished stairways and across shady verandas. I kept asking about that room. 'Will I have a room of my own?'

She turned. 'I don't think so,' and then went on to say something about it being a character-building exercise to deal with other people's issues. We had just reached the wards: six curtained beds and the doors wide open to a brightly lit corridor, the smell of disinfectant. My sister said nothing until we returned to the car. Then she said, 'You are not staying there.' In turn, I promised to see the local psychologist; promised to take the antidepressants; promised after she returned to Canada I'd let the neighbours check in and bring me parcels of food.

I didn't see you for over a month and your father, the one who couldn't organise shelves for the refrigerator, took over my shifts as well. But it's not that particular abdication that tears at my heart, it is the unspoken words I refused to let form, while feeling the full shape of them. I couldn't see you recovering lost strength. I couldn't see the colostomies reversed. I couldn't see you in a future where you would be overseeing a dazzling career. I couldn't imagine you in the future at all. I go back to that day when you were offered the operation without general anaesthetic, the day you were told your bowel was blocked and you were going to die. There were two carers, two sets of parents and four siblings standing around your bed, and the surgeon behind you, and the gastroenterologist on his knees in front begging you not to go through with this. You said you wanted to live, and I thought you were grasping a living death. I didn't believe the emergency surgery would save you, or the asparagus diet, or the cottage cheese and flaxseed, or the American shark powder drink. I wanted to take you home and tell you other sorts of lies. I wanted to buy you sugary fairy cakes. I wanted to feed you morphine.

It was your father who told me to come back, not to take over shifts or lift you onto the shower chair or blend asparagus. Just to be there.

Clemence was on duty, me a wobbly toddler perched on the side of your bed. I missed the strength in my arms and legs, my ability to lift you onto the shower chair. I had found some comfort in the rhythm of those tasks, bringing Lulu into the shower and throwing her ball while lathering you up. She'd chase it behind the cistern, skidding on the wet tiles, and sometimes I opened the door and threw the ball down the corridor, the scratchy sound of her skittering claws.

But on this day, Lulu and I waited in the room until Clemence wheeled you in wrapped in warm towels, damp hair tumbling down your back. 'So much hair,' Lillian often said, feigning annoyance. 'Why so much energy going into producing hair when it's muscle she needs.' After Clemence had brought in the shark powder drink and returned to the kitchen, you asked if I thought you were going to die. The plantation shutters were closed, sunlight like thin laser beams in the gap between each slat. I couldn't be like Lillian. I couldn't say we were going to win this battle; I wasn't sure what we were trying to win and said the only thing I knew with any certainty was we were both going to die eventually. But we weren't dead yet. We were conscious. You can't be dead in that state. No need to worry. When we were dead we'd find other coordinates and work it out from there.

Lillian was making sure you didn't die. I think she'd introduced coffee enemas by then and had started rubbing colloidal silver into your skin. She was becoming increasingly frantic as if turning left or right might be the thing that would do you in. She didn't perform these therapies in front of me but I'd seen the equipment and felt I was peeking into a previous century where physicians applied leeches to blue arms, nicked wrists and drained blood into porcelain bowls – handed them to closed-lipped maids. There was no space in which I could ask the question. *Do you want this, my dearest? Would you rather sleep?* You kept me away from the fullness of these things.

Once, when Lillian was unable to accompany you to an appointment with a specialist – which one? which one? The gastroenterologist with the faithful dog eyes or the respiratory professor of towering intellect and no ego and patient voice? – you asked Linda, the friend with the renovation business, to come in her place. Linda rang me afterwards. 'I can't believe you weren't there. I can't believe it was me hearing this news firsthand. It is clear she's reaching the end of the line. We need to get her a bigger bed so we can lie beside her in the last days.'

Did Linda use the words 'end of the line' with you? Afterwards, you didn't want her visiting. You told me she'd given up hope. Is that why you asked her to the appointment instead of me, because you didn't want me to hear the news from the specialist's mouth? There is possibility in not knowing. What did you say, my love, when you refused to attend check-ups throughout the years? 'I don't need them pointing a bone at me. I don't need their certainty. I don't need them describing how I am going to wither and die.'

So you didn't die. You lived.

But we were well past that.

I see a box frame of some sort keeping blankets from weighing on your legs. You are in the outpatient department, sleeping, the CPAP mask on your face. It is late afternoon. I can't quite remember why you are in this ward. A check-up? And why am I alone with you? The atmosphere is intimate, reminding me of the hour when I returned home from school as a girl to find the house tidy and my mother alone at the table.

A young doctor in soft shoes pulls back the beige curtain. His face is moon-shaped and young. He has a clipboard, the reports from a scan. Yes, I remember now, the whole family was coming to hear this information, but they had not yet arrived. I tell him they are coming soon. But he shares the news anyway. He tells me the tumour has grown. You stir.

'What?' you ask.

'Let's wait for Lillian,' I reply.

'No, tell me.'

And I do, as softly as if we've discovered a sleeping kitten in your bed.

You stare into space, the way I would stare into space. You whisper into your CPAP mask, 'I don't want to make any more choices.'

I pull the doctor to the side. I say, 'Her stepmother is using coffee enemas and colloidal silver back rubs. Is that helpful?'

Possibly he thinks it is me clutching for hope. 'We don't rule out alternative therapies,' he replies. 'Many approaches haven't been researched properly; it doesn't mean they might not work. People recover unexpectedly too. We don't always know why.'

Of course, of course. People buried in earthquakes, in landslides, down mine shafts have been saved by those who never gave up. Wonderful researchers were trying to find cures for cancer, cures for muscular dystrophy. They weren't giving up either.

I am such a useless thing.

Soon after you were discharged, you aspirated in your flat a second, or was it a third, time? An ambulance arrived. You returned to the hospital, your lungs siphoned, a morphine drip inserted. You were placed in a room of your own this time. Dusk outside a window. Was it the same floor where the prisoner was chained?

'Are you in pain?' I asked. You nodded. The door opened slightly, a slit of yellow light and a nurse. 'I can top up the pain relief,' she said softly.

You nodded yes.

In the corridor I caught sight of the respiratory specialist and felt free now to ask. 'Please tell me.'

'She is dying,' he said gently in that gentle evening hour in that gentle light. 'That's why we are giving her morphine. It eases her breathing.'

I wasn't there to witness what happened after I left, only that the following day I discovered you were back in your flat. Lillian said the hospital was doing nothing to try to cure you. 'We had to get her out of there. They were only offering palliative care.'

Lillian wanted you off morphine and back on track. We had to focus our efforts. She was drawing up a schedule. No point in doubling up. I should only come for my scheduled shift.

My bags had been packed for over a week, the suitcase in the boot of my car. I'd suggested to one of your carers – was it the one with the yellow ponytail? – that I thought I should come to the city full-time, sleep in the living room.

'No. You will only frighten her. Send the wrong message.'

But this time I couldn't listen to anything anyone said. I came. I texted your father on the way. Soon after, Lillian texted back. She was so angry, so disappointed. I wasn't following directions. This was not the plan.

Outside the glass doors of your block of flats I texted that if she wouldn't let me in I would sit in the café across the street. I would sit there all day. It was your father who came downstairs to buzz me up. 'Come in. Come in. Lillian is out of her head.'

I can't recall what I did upstairs. Perhaps I blended asparagus. Perhaps I sat in your room. I didn't want to get in Lillian's way. The palliative care team arrived: the doctor, a tall lanky man, and a nurse, or was it two nurses? They blend into one. Three cannulas were inserted into your back. The doctor provided instructions on when and where to insert vials of medication. I stood behind your bony haunches. He stood on the opposite side of the bed, allowing our eyes to meet. One medication to help with the pain, another to settle your breathing. Was the third a relaxant? Something in his eyes – did I imagine it? A look that suggested to me that if we used the relaxant you would fall into a sleep where you would never wake up, and I was thinking how you had whispered you didn't want to be offered any more choices, and began to pray silently that God or whoever, whatever was in charge of the universe would make this choice.

Once they were gone, Lillian gathered her equipment, was it the enema, the colloidal silver? I'm not sure, only that I was outside your room now and she went in and closed the door. Her iron will, what she could control and cure.

As for me, what was my use? What was my use? Dusk, and the café was closed. I was standing outside the glass doors of your flat when Lillian's text came through, a text that dissolved my heart.

'How do I appear to others?' she wrote, and then something about having turned into a machine, a robot.

I texted back that she looked like someone who was doing everything she could to save my daughter, and then I rang her.

'You are further ahead on this,' she said in a small voice.

I told her then about watching your grandmother die of cancer and the nurse telling me there wasn't a darn thing I could do about it.

In the bomb crater above Fismes where I'd fallen from the rim, I found myself first whispering Kipling's 'Recessional' into cupped hands. For all its annoying British imperialism and suggestion that God is some guy sitting on a throne, it still holds a central truth.

God of our fathers, known of old,

Lord of our far-flung battle-line

Beneath whose awful Hand…

Lest we forget.

A reminder of the awe-filled hand we are under, what we control and what we don't. 'God', a name for those coordinates we cannot know, and realising, in my not-knowing, that I had flung myself into space, landed on a wild beach in the Outer Hebrides, hung on to the back of a motor scooter in Kedah, and crossed a frozen railway overpass in Berlin to kiss a stranger's lips. *Lest I forget* that certainty was beyond my reach.

After your grandmother died, I spent the days leading up to her funeral eating everything in her fridge: the grapefruit she had so carefully serrated, the muffins she'd put in the freezer, the celery and thin slices of cheese on the bottom shelf. I couldn't bear to think she'd gone to the trouble of preparing the food for naught.

As for her funeral, it was a spring day filled with lilacs and maytrees in bloom. She'd been called wee May by her brothers and sister who'd been sent to the orphanage too. The children had been separated, she the youngest at four years of age – wee May, wee, wee May.

After the funeral I'd wanted to tell someone how auspicious her death had been: the scene in the hospital room so filled with grace, and suddenly realised the person I wanted to tell was her.

Now I want to tell you everything. How Lillian rang later to say she'd told you that you didn't need to fight any longer for her. How afterwards you'd fallen into a deep, deep sleep and slept better than you had in such a long, long time. At the end of the next day you died.

I sat alone in a sea of relatives from both Lillian's and your father's side. Louis and Max were not there. I think they were with Jeff. This was all too, too much for them, their sister gone and him too. I slipped into your room. It was the first time I'd seen you resting on the pillow without your CPAP mask in over fourteen years. I crouched beside you, touched your cold, folded hands and said, 'Oh, dearest,' as if there was something to be done about all of this. Out in the living room someone was boiling a kettle. Your lovely china teacups were being used.

When I came out, a funeral director had arrived and was taking notes. I felt like someone who'd met you in the dog park and dropped by to pay my respects. It was Lillian who cleared a space for me, pulled up a chair. The funeral director was gathering family information for the notice in the paper. 'And the parents?' he asked, pen in hand. Lillian pointed at your father and then at me. And this is the nub of it, you see, the pointy end that I've been wrestling with; there are so many parts. She named me as your mother and went further to suggest you be buried in the mountains close to me, how you'd liked it there. Soon after, the undertakers arrived to take you away, zipped that bag over your face. Almost everyone followed the trolley down in the elevator. I can't remember why. Perhaps to open the security doors in the parking lot, perhaps to move cars. Your father and I remained in your room, shell-shocked and staring. He suddenly said, 'Do you remember it was a broken condom?'

Of course I remembered, and it was such a gift to know these funny memories were not mine alone. It had been Christmas. Christopher was only three months old.

'Yes, I remember,' I said. 'And when she was born you said with delight, *Oh, it's a little girl.*'

And then he put his arms around me and said, 'There, there.'

It was the first time I'd been touched since your death. No one had placed their arms around me until then, and here I was being held in the arms of one who had been the enemy for so many years.

Of course skirmishes followed. There was no way your father would agree to Jeff coming anywhere near the funeral. 'He deserted you! He deserted my daughter! A drive-by on his bicycle is as close as he gets.'

But how could Louis and Max come to your funeral under those conditions? I was torn right down the middle – whose side, whose side – and feeling this war had grown out of me, out of the slums of Glasgow, out of a mutated egg, out of generations of poor people told to use the back door, pinching pennies from counters – those people, that person, the sinful, sinful girl whose baby had just been zipped into a bag. She could only be returned to me like this. She'd borne my sin. It's a woman's body that bears the sin.

I was babbling these things in the hollow above Fismes, telling Hermie everything: why I'd come to France in the first place, why I needed to see Section E. Why I had only been able to see the Writers Walk because I'd been stung with nettles first. I was no warrior or poet. I should be shot at dawn. As for Lillian, her kindness in pointing to me, saying I was your mother.

Hermie pulled me to my feet. 'Lillian didn't award you that position; she was simply stating a fact. Brush yourself off. I need to show you something.'

By then the sky was tremendous, glowing pink and grey. The sun had started to set. I could feel my heart sloshing about in the tin cage of my chest as Hermie marched me down the hill and back to the car. He handed me the keys. 'Your journey,' he said. 'I'll give directions. Need to see it again myself because I think I'll make better sense of it, having listened to you.'

We drove into a thinly gathering dark. I think we crossed a small bridge, the shadow of a wood on one side. 'Stop here,' he said. I pulled into a grassy swale. There was a gate, a patch of gravel, a low wall. I picked my way over the gravel. It took a moment to make sense of it but slowly in the gloom the shapes took form: rows of crosses. As I drew closer I could see they were made out of hammered metal, the dullest gleam, and not very high. It was a German graveyard, the crosses engraved with names of young men, mostly young, the ones on the wrong side who possibly hadn't wanted to be on anyone's side either and had lost. No triumphalism here, and because of that I could kneel down sobbing and say, 'I know, I know. And I am so terribly sorry.'

Marne Region,
north-eastern France
9 October 2017

I have been cleaning Sylvie's cottage, although I won't leave until tomorrow. Tonight I will have dinner with Carole and Arnaud.

Hermie left earlier this morning. He served me French toast for breakfast. In France they refer to it as *pain perdu*: lost bread. The French don't eat it for breakfast, perhaps for afternoon tea or dessert. He placed the dish in front of me in an authoritative way, like an efficient nurse or the military in action feeding rations to the troops. He will stay at his own lodgings tonight and from there fly back to America. He sat at the table sorting out travel details and sending emails, and then packed his car and drove away. I don't think we hugged.

I got into my car as he got into his, didn't go anywhere in particular – just drove a little way through fields of yellow rapeseed and then turned back. I didn't want Hermie leaving and me waving a kerchief at the door.

It was the same a year ago in Berlin. I had to be out of my flat in the morning but wasn't due at the airport until much later in the day. I went over to Hermie's room at the artists residency to wait out those few hours. I think he offered me some marmalade on toast and then I sat at my laptop to finalise travel arrangements and send emails too. He left me for a while and then came behind my chair and kissed the back of my neck. There is something about Hermie when he comes up behind me in this way that makes me feel as if I've been lifted onto the handlebars of a mischievous boy's bike and taken down to a creek. He pulled me onto the bed.

Afterwards, we lay silent underneath the bit of cloth over the window that turned the room pink, and then after that, emerged into the ordinary afternoon light, dragging my ordinary suitcase to the ordinary bus stop and to the airport from there. On the way, we crossed over the railway overpass where we first met. Lovers had fastened locks onto the rusting fence rails. I couldn't understand the graffiti, but it was something about love, something about forever.

At Berlin airport I told him it was silly to wait, no point dragging out farewells. I may have hugged him lightly that time but could feel he was keen to get away too. Perhaps like me he didn't want to witness the end of things. When I was a girl I tried to make moments stop, thought if I stared long enough at the afternoon sun it couldn't turn into evening. I'd thought the same that afternoon when Clemence brought you to your room after your shower, the slanting sunlight, the decals on your window, your hair curling over your back. Just don't blink and this will be forever and ever.

On that beach on the wild island in the Outer Hebrides, twilight turned the ivory sand pale blue; Venus rose. The bleached driftwood took on a ghostly glow. Again I was trying so hard to watch everything carefully, hoping it might stay this beautiful. Twilight might never end, but it did.

Your father rang six months after you died. He began in that abrupt way he does.

'Where are you?'

I'd been working in my home office and was still in my pyjamas. 'Here,' I replied, feeling confused. His question was like an accusation. Where did he expect me to be?

'Good. I'm in the car. I'll meet you at the Commonwealth Bank.'

'Which Commonwealth Bank?'

'The one in your town.'

'Is there a Commonwealth Bank in my town?'

'Jesus, there's a Commonwealth Bank in every town.'

I knew he was probably correct and said I would find it, and yes meet him there. I googled the address and when it came up on the screen realised I'd walked past it countless times. I hadn't asked why I was supposed to meet him there; he was off the phone before I could. I arrived first and waited.

He came in carrying Lulu. He always has Lulu with him now, takes her to his office and out to restaurants, sits at a table outside if they won't let her in. She's a little bit fat.

'Oh, hi,' he said brushing past me and heading for the information counter. I joined him as he slapped down documents. Among them was your death certificate. I hadn't seen it yet. A rush came over me, the same rush when I had tried to imagine you in a grave and couldn't, although the marker is there now, under a great eucalyptus tree, its sage leaves feathered above. There'd been some toing and froing about the location of your plot, Lillian being Catholic, and you having been confirmed Catholic under her care. She had wanted to cross religious divisions as she wandered through the cemetery, had said the Anglican side looked a little smarter. But Catholic priests don't officiate in Anglican sections, even as they bend to conduct ceremonies in Independent areas.

So now you lie in the Independent section of the cemetery close to wild bushland. We have planted thyme and a rose bearing your name, and pansies. A terracotta dish collects water, a small bird modelled on its lip. You liked movies where girls in long stockings carry flowers to graves holding the hand of an older woman wearing a hat. So I go there, wearing a hat with a slanted brim.

Your funeral was conducted in the little convict church across from your flat. It was so crowded people had to stand outside. Lillian chose the hymns, which included the Anglican version of 'The Lord Is My Shepherd' because she didn't want me to feel left out. She also worried about people singing, not only that song but the others. 'Catholics don't sing as enthusiastically as Protestants,' she said, and so we asked a young singer, a friend of Louis, if she could lead. She agreed but then tearfully confessed she was Buddhist and was having difficulty with such unfamiliar songs.

'What will we do?' Lillian rang the night before. 'The service has been printed!'

'We're going to lead them,' I replied.

She was horrified. 'Begin singing alone! That would frighten me to death.'

'It will frighten me to death too,' I replied, and could hear you laughing. Lillian and I researched YouTube versions and practised that night.

In the church I sat with your brothers and my friends wearing your purple dress. Everyone on that side of the church was wearing purple in honour of the colour you loved. Your father and Lillian, honouring another sense of decorum, sat on the opposite side with their friends and family dressed smartly in black. When the moment came to sing, I stood up, because that's what you do in Anglican churches, and then realised everyone else was still sitting down. Lillian crossed the aisle, put her arm around my waist and so like that we began.

Your father had chosen 'Goodnight, My Angel' for the recessional hymn. He had been listening to it when Lillian told him it was the last time he would kiss his daughter goodnight, and everything had to be perfect. Her brothers and mother must be there, and so Jeff was there too, at the back, Max keeping guard. Christopher arrived from Western Australia where he lives now, and your eldest half-brother from Canada, and Lillian and your father's shy-eyed son, and your godson, and your sister of course. It was those young men who rose and clasped one another's hands under the casket to shoulder you out.

The woman at the information counter in the Commonwealth Bank turned the form around.

'That's my daughter's death certificate,' said your father, holding Lulu. 'She wasn't married, no children. I'm her father.' He nodded towards me. 'And this is her mother. We've been happily divorced for over thirty years. We need the money released from our daughter's account to pay the carers' bill.'

Of course, your account had been with the Commonwealth Bank, your government allowance deposited there. How many times had you handed me the card, told me to run to the shop for something, given me the PIN over and over because I forget numbers?

The woman behind the counter said kindly that she would be back.

'Oh gawd,' I whispered. 'This is so hard.'

Your father agreed and offered to buy me a cup of coffee afterwards, and so afterwards I sat in the sunshine outside a café with Lulu, while he stood in the line-up buying coffee and chocolate cake. He can't help buying cake. He brought the tray to the table and bent to give a piece to Lulu. I slapped at his hand. 'Chocolate can kill little dogs,' I said.

He remembered, and gasped. 'I've been having trouble sleeping,' he said. 'Keep waking up. I've been forgetting the routine for the CPAP machine. Do you remember the routine? The sticky pads on her nose and the sides of her mouth first, the face washer over her head and ears, and then pulling the velcro straps to the right position, putting tissues in the cracks? I dream I'm doing that and can't remember the order.' He turned to me with a desperate expression. 'I'm forgetting the order.' He took a breath and began again. 'I've been seeing a counsellor. We talk about lots of things. I told her about how I went to Western Australia when I was eighteen. That's how I made the money to go overseas, how I met you. But I didn't fit the mines; I was a really small, weedy guy. I've always been trying to find my tribe.'

I thought then of the boy I'd met all those years ago, the crushed velvet flares, his love of art. He moved to feed Lulu again but checked himself. 'I know it was awful,' he said, meaning your illness. 'But I don't think she was ever lonely.' He stared into space, seeing all of it. I was seeing all of it too. The effort. All the effort. The asparagus diet, the chandelier hanging in the bathroom, Lulu chasing a ball in and out of the shower. You laughing. Jeff lifting you onto a table in an operating room.

'I don't always get things right,' said your father, breaking into my thoughts. 'Still can't figure out where I belong. My tribe.'

Lulu was watching him. He picked her up and then repeated that despite not getting things perfect or knowing his tribe, where he fit in, he didn't think you were ever lonely.

The disease was terrible, but you were never alone. And then as if he had recognised something comforting, he added, 'At least I'm the guy who always shows up.'

'Yes,' I replied. 'You always showed up.'

In England, near Alrewas in Staffordshire, three hundred and nine wooden stakes stand behind a blindfolded soldier. It is a memorial to disgraced servicemen executed by firing squad during World War I. The installation was approved in 2006 by the then Defence Secretary, Des Browne. He was reversing a previous decision made in 1993 when Prime Minister John Major had been adamant that such soldiers should not be pardoned, never mind honoured in this way. These men had been deserters. Cowards. Too frightened to stay and fight. It would be an insult to those who had died honourably on the battlefield or had been exonerated in a fair trial.

Browne countered that he didn't want to second-guess decisions made by commanders in the battlefields or military courts. However, it was clear all of these men had been victims of war.

I have been thinking about that monument as I sit at Sylvie's table, mist tumbling in the fields beyond. A lone bird swoops. I'm also thinking about the time when I returned to Canada a few years ago. I'd been invited to your eldest half-brother's wedding. I met his adoptive parents at a dinner organised by his fiancée's mother. She is a sweet woman, teaches at a primary school, and was so pleased to have the birth mother and adoptive mother in the same room.

'I wished I'd toasted you both,' she said later.

I smiled in response but was relieved she hadn't. It was enough we were all in the room, all that complexity swirling around. It wasn't my son's adoptive mother's fault I'd been put in a position where I'd signed a form saying I'd never have knowledge of him again. But to toast us both would have signalled an all-encompassing victory, as if this was the planned end of a story, all things leading in this direction, and the only thing to be understood.

As for you. As for this time in France. Through Sylvie's window I see the garden shrouded in fog but every so often light breaks through the mist. Patches in the distant fields glimmer, suggesting there is something further away for me to see. I think it is the most that can be said of this journey: complexity shot through with fleeting light and love. Always love, my dearest. Always love.

Acknowledgements

A writer may compose alone in a room but it takes a team to bring a book into the world.

My team includes those who read the first raw pages: the ever-sensitive and insightful Peter Bishop who saw what I was doing; and Vanessa Kirkpatrick and Vicki Laveau-Harvie who encouraged me too. Dear friends Katerina Cosgrove, Loubna Haikal, Victoria Bramwell-Davis, Jill and Ian McGilvray, and Stephen Measday were wonderful sounding boards for the first complete draft.

I am also grateful to those who read the manuscript with an editorial eye prior to submission: Mark O'Flynn and Jessie Cole for their thoughts on structure, and Catherine Therese who did the same and more. Her depth of understanding sustained me as I pressed on.

To Michelle Rickerby and Shane Porteous, thank you for coming into my life at just the right moment. Michelle for encouraging me to submit, for getting me back in touch with the voice of this story and for directing the audio production of the book. Shane, where would I be without your dramatic coaching? My heartfelt thanks.

I would also like to thank Valerie Huston for her help with French vernacular, even as my stilted schoolgirl pronunciation remains.

I am ever grateful to Bronwyn Mehan, publisher, curator and producer at Spineless Wonders. Bronwyn has made it her mission to bring new voices into the world and to foster the development of young editors, designers and producers. Among her assembled team I thank Rose Sammut for her forensic editing eye, Oliver Agbisit for his tech support in recording the audio version of this book, and Bettina Kaiser for designing a print version with skill and sensitivity.

I would also like to thank Susan McCreery, proofreader extraordinaire. Sue, if there is a mistake in the print version it is my fault not yours.

My sister Alice, my brother David and the rest of my family believed in me and kept me fed when times grew lean. I love you all so very much.

Finally, I want to acknowledge someone whom I have never met, Rudolf Binding, the soldier whose letter appears at the beginning of this book. I found Binding's letter when I was searching websites for letters written in WWI. His letter resonated so deeply it stopped me in my tracks. Later, after finishing the manuscript, I discovered he was a German writer who studied medicine. Someone on the other side. His diary and letters, *A Fatalist at War*, were published in 1927. His collected war poems, stories and recollections were published after his death in 1938.

Author's Biography

Carol Major was born in Scotland, was educated in Canada and finally settled in the Blue Mountains of Australia, a place that reflects all three landscapes and where she has been able to write herself home.

Carol's short stories and poems have been published in Canadian and Australian journals. She has also written extensively in the health care and social policy field. She continues to freelance and provides mentoring services to authors at Varuna, Australia's National Writers House.

www.ingramcontent.com/pod-product-compliance
Lightning Source LLC
Chambersburg PA
CBHW021144080526
44588CB00008B/210